Container Gardening

COLLECTION MANAGEMENT

Container Gardening

Kathy Brown

THE CROWOOD PRESS

First published in 2011 by
The Crowood Press Ltd
Ramsbury, Marlborough
Wiltshire SN8 2HR

www.crowood.com

British Library Cataloguing-in-Publication Data
A catalogue record for this book is available from the British Library.

ISBN 978 1 84797 275 0

Dedication
To my father-in-law, Peter Brown OBE

Acknowledgements
I would like to acknowledge the kindness of Pat Russell and Ute Brock, John Taylor 2 of O.A. Taylor & Sons Bulbs Ltd., and Neil Lucas from Knoll Gardens. Also Harrod Horticultural for such excellent vegetable containers and Henry Richardson Designs for the slatted wooden container wraps and obelisk. I would also like to thank my cousin Vanessa Kay of www.vanessakayphotography.co.uk for taking such stunning photos of succulents.

Frontispiece
Raised containers add a whole new dimension to planting schemes. Here an old Afghan rice pot is home to a dainty mix of orchids, pink *Erigeron* 'Dimity', silver-leaved *Festuca glauca* and yellow *Sedum reflexum*. Japanese Blood Grass *Imperata cylindrica rubra*, and pretty white and pink Mexican daisy *Erigeron karvinskianus* are planted in the lower pot.

635.986

Typeset by Jean Cussons Typesetting, Diss, Norfolk

Printed and bound in China by Everbest Printing Co Ltd

CONTENTS

PREFACE

Container gardening is exciting because the opportunities are boundless. And fortunately the container garden is forever expandable from floor to wall, so there is always room for additions. Moreover, the choice of plants is vast. Each season can bring different combinations and colour schemes. There will always be a new plant to try or a new pot to plant.

So much fun can be had in planting up the unexpected – an old shoe, a telephone, a redundant satellite dish, a set of scales – anything that will hold soil or compost, just so long as there is a hole for drainage. Micro gardening has its place too, with a spoon recommended for planting up mini egg containers instead of a trowel. Even the first-time gardener can have wonderful results with a simple window box, pots beside the front door or a whole balcony or patio decked out with containers.

This book contains lots of traditional ideas for both summer and winter pots – one-season planting schemes which are bold and rewarding. It also includes many suggestions for growing food in containers, whether fruit, vegetables, herbs or flowers; in their own way they all help to create 'an instant supermarket' for use in the kitchen and without the environmental concern about air miles. Many of the schemes, however, are for long-term containers, which will continue to give pleasure as well as saving both work and money. Some require overwintering in a greenhouse, such as begonias, pelargoniums and fuchsias, but many include hardy plants which will stand the test of winter weather outside and may well improve as they mature.

The selection of containers and plants, and their placement, can be used to create dramatically different effects. A little pot, planted with the same bulbs, repeated several times, will bring harmony and strength; this is also true of larger containers. Imagine three or four hanging baskets arranged against a sunny wall of a balcony, house or garage. As summer baskets filled with plants of the same glorious colour they are both uplifting and sumptuous. If the wall is in partial shade where hostas will thrive, you could plant each basket with a hosta surrounded by fillers and trailers such as the creeping jenny, violas or mimulus, and you suddenly have a hardy year-round scheme which will last for many years, with the violas and mimulus self-seeding.

In each section of the book there are planting combinations for different types of plants; keep in mind that they are suggestive rather than prescriptive, showing the range of possibilities. The step-by-step recipes given in Chapter 8 are for both short-term and long-term containers using bulbs, bedding plants, succulents, vegetables, grasses and shrubs. They offer a list of ingredients, method of planting and aftercare, and you can of course alter the ingredients to suit your own preferences. Finally a calendar of care is provided to give you reminders throughout the year on how to keep your garden containers fresh and healthy.

There is so much room for experimentation with containers. Ultimately the choices are yours, and what variety to choose from! Participating is half the buzz, and there is just so much to enjoy.

OPPOSITE: **Micro gardening: baby succulents make fascinating shapes in these planted eggshells.**

1 THE BASICS

CHOICE OF PLANTS

Hardiness

One of the first details to be aware of when buying plants for containers is whether they are hardy or tender. Plant hardiness is a measure of the lowest temperature that a plant can survive during the winter. The Royal Horticultural Society recognizes four categories in the United Kingdom: H denotes the plant being fully hardy to –15°C (5°F); FH = Frost Hardy, withstanding temperatures down to –5°C (23°F); HH = only Half Hardy, surviving at temperatures no lower than 0°C (32°F); and FT = Frost Tender, which means that it cannot survive less than 5°C (41°F).

Note, however, that these RHS categories relate to plants in soil, not in containers. Planting in containers results in greater exposure to cold temperatures, since the whole plant, including its roots, is above ground. In pots, the frost will penetrate the compost more easily and freeze it solid, whereas in the borders maybe only the top 5–8cm of soil will be frozen unless extremely cold conditions are endured. Hardy plants can be kept outside on your patio through the winter; any other plant will need protection unless you live in a very sheltered spot near the coast or in a warmer metropolitan heat island where the temperatures are usually several degrees higher than the country areas.

OPPOSITE: **Both little and large pots are excellent for use in the garden.**

RIGHT: **Hardy winter-flowering bulbs have been planted in these shallow pots where they will survive unscathed by cold weather.**

Frost hardy plants might survive without a greenhouse if you bubble-wrap the pots themselves, ensuring some protection for the roots, compost and containers. Meanwhile, fleece jackets can be used as protection for the plants, allowing light and moisture to penetrate the material. The jackets will have a chord to tie around the trunk of the plant to keep them in place in windy conditions. Their main benefit is to trap and retain the warmer daytime heat by putting on the cover in early afternoon. In times of freezing daytime temperatures, however, there will be no benefit.

Moving them to a safer site during winter is also helpful. Place the pots against a south-facing house wall where they are able to take advantage of the heat escaping from the bricks. Better still, place them on a south-facing outdoor window sill. Or put them under cover of an awning or veranda where the cover will help to save some of the heat loss. An unheated potting shed or garage will also be of benefit if there is a window to let in the light. Keeping them dry will help too. Wet containers in heavy frosts are bad news for any but fully hardy plants. With any of these actions you will still be in the danger zone where frost hardy plants are concerned, but taking measures

to keep them is certainly worth a try, as no winter is quite like another.

The half hardy plants need full protection. An unheated greenhouse in a sheltered location might be enough to see them through, especially if all the plants are kept on the dry side – bring the pots into the greenhouse in the autumn and don't water again until early spring. When you see new signs of life with buds and shoots appearing, water sparingly at first and then more regularly as temperatures rise and growth is greater. In severe weather, where temperatures are consistently freezing for days and weeks, heat will be necessary. You can find a device with a thermostat which will control the temperature and only activate when a certain minimum is reached. These are guidelines only – experience will vary. In my garden fifty miles north of London, in an open country spot, none of the plants mentioned in this book have had more protection than being kept just frost free. So even though *Fuchsia*

'Thalia' is described as being Frost Tender by some growers, it has survived in temperatures no warmer than that of the frost-free greenhouse. Being kept in fairly dry compost certainly helps. To be safe, offer the frost tender plants a minimum of 5°C.

If you don't have a greenhouse you can still enjoy a patio bursting with colour and foliage interest. For the tender plants, it means you will have to start afresh each season. Buy them and enjoy them for one summer. You will be able to keep the hardy shrubs, perennials and grasses so you can have a core of background pots. In addition you can grow lots of annuals which can be sown in spring. This give you a blaze of colour not only for your ornamental containers but for your kitchen containers as well, with many vegetables falling into this category, such as salad leaves, peas, French and runner beans, beetroot and carrots. These can all be sown in spring to give bumper summer crops. With a greenhouse

Seeds of many annual plants can be sown direct in late spring without the need of a greenhouse, including salad leaves, beans, spring onions, beetroots and carrots.

or sunny indoor windowsill you can also have tomatoes, courgettes and sweetcorn. But if you want to skip this sowing stage you can easily find young plants to buy. Plant them straight into their summer containers towards the end of spring when risk of frost has passed.

For the Season or Long Term?

The choice of plants is tantalizing, whether they are for just one season colour or long-term appreciation. For the short term, you might fill your autumn and spring window box and pots with pansies, sweetly scented violas mixed with pink or red *Bellis perennis* daisies. They will bring lovely bright colour for several weeks but sadly they won't survive through the rest of the year, though the violas might seed. The same is true with many of the summer bedding plants. A hanging basket with trailing petunias will bring three months of colour but then come to an end.

However, a hanging basket with a fern or hosta will live for years. Plant shrubs such as mahonia, holly and hydrangea and you will have pots which just get better and better as they grow and mature. Treat them as investment plants and with occasional repotting you can enjoy them for a decade or more. The joy of container gardening is that you can appreciate both kinds of plants. Some pots and baskets can have instant colour, with the joy of changing the mix year on year. While larger pots can host the long term schemes and provide the backbone to the patio.

Colour or Form?

Another area for choice is whether to grow for colour or form. The summer bedding plants such as lobelia, tagetes, busy lizzies, nasturtiums and geraniums, and summer bulbs such as begonias and lilies will all give a massive display of bright colour, with a rich choice of blues, pinks, yellows and reds. These you can mix and match to your heart's content, until you find your favourite combination – or you could go on experimenting forever, such is the choice. Rather than high colour, you could opt for a quieter look using all

A hanging basket with *Petunia Surfinia* and *Scaevola* provides instant summer colour, but for one season only (although the scaevola should survive with the help of greenhouse protection).

A hanging basket with *Athyrium filix-femina* the female fern and *Lysimachia nummularia* 'Aurea' golden Creeping Jenny creates a long-term basket.

Shapes can be just as important as colour in containers, especially if you are able to echo one plant with another. The dome of the *Dasylirion* matches the *Cordyline* and *Stipas* (right).

whites for example, such as white daffodils with white dicentra and white sweet woodruff, pretty as individuals but even better as a group, and especially good if you place them against a dark background.

Alternatively you might prefer the emphasis on form provided by foliage. Ferns, grasses, hostas, cordylines and succulents will all offer fascinating shapes and patterns, which is reward enough without the flowers. Where the flowers do appear then they are a bonus rather than the main player.

Edible Plants

A kitchen garden can be planted in a hanging basket, a window box or free standing raised beds with herbs, vegetables, fruit and edible flowers ready for picking at a moment's notice. The sunnier the site the better, but whether it is a step

or a short walk, the benefits of growing your own are immense: no chemicals, no air miles, just fresh tasty produce with an ever increasing choice. So much opportunity exists with a vast array of seeds available, many of them heirloom varieties. There is also scope for a quick succession of crops lasting from late spring right through to late autumn. Although the mid to late summer months will be the high point, certain herbs such as sage, thyme, bay and rosemary will keep their leaves all year round and can be picked and used at will.

CONTAINERS

Almost any receptacle can be used if it has drainage holes. There is a wonderful variety of heavyweight slate, granite and marble, medium-weight wood and terracotta, and lightweight fibreglass and basketry which will all give a different character to your garden, from sleek and minimalist to rustic and cottagey.

Winter frosts can cause damage to the fabric of containers, with flaking and even splitting of terracotta pots. Look out for the frost proof guarantee against the damage of frost, and keep all your receipts. Fewer problems seem to occur with glazed terracotta pots, which are fired to a higher temperature and are therefore less porous. In addition the glazing prevents moisture entering from the outside. On the other hand some pots are unashamedly not frost proof and will be suitable for tender plants which are kept indoors or in a greenhouse during the winter.

Check the size of the drainage hole(s) at the base of a pot. They should be 1.5cm or more across. Where they are too small, the roots will clog up the hole leaving the pot like a sink with the plug in, which is bad news at any time but

Empty eggshells planted with tiny succulents are great fun and cost virtually nothing.

The pot has split due to excessive pressure from the agave roots; re-potting was long overdue.

particularly so in frosty weather. Plenty of drainage material on top of the hole will help, topped by a layer of fabric membrane, sacking or a 'J cloth' to stop the roots reaching down into this area. Raising the container off the ground with pot holders or bricks will also assist drainage.

Another cause of breakage is keeping the plant in too small a pot. An agave will put on massive root growth and if not moved on into larger pots will eventually break the one it has been in for a number of years.

References to pot sizes can be confusing as every manufacturer will have their own thoughts on small, medium and large. To make matters more difficult pots can have the same width but different depths. Small pots in this book are deemed to be less than 30cm in height and diameter; medium pots are up to 45cm in height and diameter with large pots being anything greater.

TOP LEFT: **A straight-sided, flat-bottomed pot will give stability to a planting scheme with a tall specimen such as a standard holly or bay, or shrub roses.**

TOP RIGHT: **Use a false inner container to plant up a large beehive pot.**

Using some quirky planters adds hugely to the fun of container gardening. You just have to match the plants to the growing space available. Succulents are great in a shallow container. Hardy little house leeks *Sempervivium* are fine in an old shoe with some holes in the bottom or even an empty egg shell for the summer months; after this you might have to replant. Tender *Echeveria* can also be planted if you can offer them winter protection on an indoor window sill.

If you are choosing a pot for a planting scheme you know you are going to repot every year or so, then don't be tempted to buy pots with a narrow opening or with a waist beneath the rim, as this makes emptying the pot out very difficult. It is so much easier to use a straight-sided pot or a flared one.

When choosing a pot for a tall planting scheme for a shrub or standard plant like a holly or bay,

where the top growth acts like a sail, avoid ones which are curved at the bottom – always choose a pot with a solid flat base which makes it far more stable.

Where you have a tall chimney pot, a large Ali Baba or beehive pot, you might prefer to use a more shallow inner plastic pot that sits snugly in the top of the container as your planting pot. It saves on the cost of the soil and makes seasonal changeovers easy. You might plant up a second identical inner pot, say a hardy arrangement of bulbs and trailing ivies, so it will be ready to take the place of the previous season's more tender display, which can then be protected through the winter ready to reappear, more mature, the following summer.

Hanging baskets are a popular means of growing plants suspended in mid air. One of the major drawbacks, however, is that the plants dry out very quickly, especially when using moss-lined wire baskets. Wicker hanging baskets with a plastic lining are far easier to plant and look after. Remember, the larger the basket, the greater the volume of soil and the bigger the root area, which means a potentially better display. The 36cm diameter baskets are excellent, but the next size up, the 41cm diameter baskets, are even better. You will need a longer bracket for the bigger baskets. Often when you hang up the basket it is facing the wrong direction. Well, it can of course be changed 180 degrees by simply hanging it the other way round. But if you want a quarter turn then simply use a butcher's S hook on the bracket; these are normally available from a hardware shop. Not only does it give you extra flexibility with the position, but it also lowers the basket. If possible avoid baskets which are too high, as they are difficult to water and show off their bottoms rather than their main display. It is far better to 'look into' your basket at eye level, to smell the flowers, to appreciate the colours, to crop the vegetables or whatever. Lower baskets are easier to tend and enjoy.

SITE

Plant labels often refer to a plant's preference for sun or shade, or partial shade. Of course there will be some days when the sun does not shine at all because of cloud cover, but full sun is regarded as having at least 6 full hours of direct sunlight. Some plants would bask in sunshine all day and every day; this is just a minimum requirement. Partial sun refers to a site having 3–6 hours of sunshine each day, preferably in the morning and early afternoon; partial shade will have the same number of hours of sunshine but without the full afternoon heat. Full shade means less than 3 hours of direct sunshine each day with filtered light the rest of the day. This labelling helps us to choose the right plant for the right place. Thankfully, many plants will enjoy conditions both in full sun and partial shade.

Many plants will grow better in sheltered conditions. An exposed roof terrace is obviously a difficult spot. So too is the passageway between houses, or between a house and garage. Here the passage acts as a wind tunnel, with the consequent turbulent conditions and cooler air. Try to create shelter if possible by means of a glass panel on a roof terrace or balcony, or a gate to the passageway.

The spot for the patio should be chosen, if possible, where the sun can warm it up and it is out of the way of persistent breezes. Plant a hedge or maybe erect a pergola or trellis as a shield to a windy patio; soon plants will grow up it and filter the wind. If space allows have a secondary smaller terrace, even just a bench or barbeque table on a few paving stones or gravel, where the evening

Lagurus ovatus produces dainty flower spikes, turning from pale green to creamy white with very soft long awns, hence the common name of bunny tails or hare's tail. It is raised up on the table to catch the low evening sunlight with *Carex dolichostachya* 'Kaga-nishiki' behind it.

sunlight can be enjoyed. Place some pots of grasses such as *Lagurus ovatus* (illustrated on page 15) on the table and add backlighting for dramatic effect – fleeting maybe, but it is worth trying to capture, if your situation allows it.

If your balcony or patio is in shade however, don't despair – there are many plants which will cope with these conditions. You can enjoy foliage shapes and textures from ferns and ivies, while many of the shade-loving flowering plants have white flowers which show up beautifully in the darker areas. Try plants to see how they will cope – a plant in the wrong place won't necessarily die, it just won't thrive as well. Shiny surfaces on glazed pots and an outdoor mirror to act like a false sun will also help to brighten the scene. Create your own mood; shady and sheltered can be a satisfying part of the garden.

Sometimes containers can be used to distract from ugly features like drain covers and rainwater pipes. A large pot can sit on a drain cover and completely disguise the metal or plastic cover; similarly a hanging basket or even better a two-tier hanging basket can take the eye from an ugly drainpipe.

NURTURING

Compost

Multi-purpose compost is the usual type of compost used for summer bedding plants. It is lightweight and easy to use. In recent years the peat content has been reduced, with extra material such as bark, coir, green compost and wood waste used instead. Peat-free composts are also available.

For all winter work and long-term schemes, a soil-based compost is preferable as it offers better sustainability and better drainage over a longer period: John Innes No2 formula is recommended

Decorative glass on top of a mulching mat are attractive and practical for a single stem shrub or succulent such as this *Echeveria* 'Gypsy'; the mat helps to prevent soil splash on the glass.

for bulbs and established plants, while John Innes No 3 is recommended for mature shrubs and trees. Where acid-loving plants are grown then ericaceous compost, which omits lime, must be used. It can be purchased as a multi-purpose and a soil-based compost.

Mulches

Topping the container with a mulch is practical and also looks good. Horticultural grit or pebbles, coloured glass, bark or moss can all have their advantages. Any of the mulches will help to avoid water loss through evaporation at the top of the container. A thick layer of bark will assist in

OPPOSITE: **A shady part of the garden is lifted by brightly coloured begonias and a large outdoor mirror, while rainbow coloured plastic slinky springs add their own touch of magic.**

Crushed seashells provide a light mulch for a single specimen planting scheme allowing new shoots to emerge, as with this star sedge *Rhynchospora latifolia.*

keeping out frost from the top of the container. A good covering of grit or other hard material might deter mice or squirrels from pilfering newly planted autumn bulbs.

Where you have only one plant in the pot, say a succulent or a tree, consider a mulch which will enhance the look of the container. First lay some porous plant membrane on top of the soil to prevent soil splash. Then place your pebbles or glass beads on top and enjoy the effect.

Where you have a plant which will send up lots of shoots, then simply lay a light mulch such as grit or crushed shells. Where you have a scarcity of plants such as a snowdrop hanging basket, then adding bark or fir cones will enhance the composition. In the summertime when bedding plants are used, however, mulch will be superfluous; they grow so quickly that they will soon cover the top of the container and the mulch will not be seen.

Feed

Multi-purpose compost normally has enough food ingredients for the first four to six weeks of the life of a newly planted container. Thereafter it will need help. So you could include a long-term pelleted food mixed in with the compost at the time of planting which will slowly release nutrients over the next few months; this should take you right through a summer season. Otherwise, after the initial four to six weeks, simply apply a regular water-soluble feed; at the height of the summer growing season this might be every week or two – try and make it a regular evening of the week, then you will remember when it should be done. With all long-term planting schemes, except the succulents, it helps to use a general-purpose feed in spring; apply it at soil level being careful to avoid contact with any foliage. You will need to rely on a liquid feed the following summer. Repeat the procedure in subsequent years.

Water

Water is vital to container gardening. Without it nothing will grow, although demands of plants will vary; succulents need much less than petunias, for example, which will soon flag if they are thirsty; and thirsty plants are quick to get attacked by aphids. So water awareness helps to ensure plant health. A simple check using the finger test can be made regularly to assess the moisture content of the soil. If you put your finger into the soil to a depth of around 5cm and it comes out with soil lightly attached, everything is good. If it comes out clean, the soil is too dry. If it comes out with wet soil attached it is too wet.

Daily watering in hot weather will ensure healthy plants (apart from succulents which can be watered much less often). It is best to water in the early morning or evening when the sun is not directly on the plants, as otherwise the leaves will scorch to the detriment of plant growth and looks. It is also best to water at soil level, not on top of the plant. This will ensure that the soil receives the moisture, rather than its being wasted by running off the leaves to the ground. It also means that you don't drown the flowers of plants. Petunias for example do not like being sprayed with water. One plant that does like a regular misting in hot weather, however, is the fuchsia; here a daily misting above and watering below will be well rewarded.

Acid loving plants growing in ericaceous compost will prefer rain water to tap water, which contains lime. If you want to grow camellias, skimmias and rhododendrons for example then be sure to have an adequate water butt which will capture the rain water.

Generally, plants growing in a soil-based compost will cope better with dry weather than those growing in a multi-purpose compost which dries out quicker. This is one reason why water-retaining crystals are often incorporated into multi-purpose compost at the time of planting.

Glazed pots are impervious and retain the moisture far better than ordinary terracotta pots.

Self-watering pots have a reservoir at the base which is fed by a tube which rises above the compost level; the plastic surround is impervious so it helps to retain moisture and makes watering more effective.

Summer vacations can present a problem for containers. A weekend might not make any difference, especially if it rains, but a two-week period without watering would be tricky. Either ask a friend to do the watering or use an automatic watering system. Some watering systems can be set up with an automatic watering and feeding regime regulated by a timer. If none of these are possible then move the containers into a shady, sheltered part of the garden where there will be less stress on the plants. Succulents can survive for a week or so without the need for irrigation.

Winter can pose other water problems both to the plants and the pots as already discussed above.

Supports

Plant supports for tall vegetables such as runner beans and cucumbers, as well as for roses and clematis, are a necessary addition to the container, unless you can place the container near a wall and let the plants grow up a trellis fixed to the wall. A few tall bamboo canes tied together at the top with string is a simple solution for annual climbers. A readymade metal or basketry support inserted into container will be longer lasting, and will be more stable if a deep container is used. Check the width at the bottom of the support to make sure it fits in the container. Fine wire work can also offer a good solution if you can find a tall cylindrical shape.

PESTS

Healthy plants are far less likely to be attacked by aphids such as greenfly, white fly or black fly, so the number one priority is to keep containers well fed and watered. If a build-up of such pests occurs, you might hope that other insects and birds will be nearby to feast on them. Other help is at hand by means of various organic and inorganic sprays if you want to take the more proactive route.

Certain bugs will cause serious problems. Vine weevil (*Otiorhynchus sulcatus*) is the curse of many containers. The hard shiny black beetles eat the leaves of plants, while the little creamy white

Each tiny dry water-retaining crystal absorbs 400–500 times its weight in water, and when hydrated it turns into a gel which acts as a reservoir for the plant roots. Daily watering is still recommended in hot weather, but as they take longer to dry out the plants will no longer flag, thereby ensuring much healthier plants.

Ordinary terracotta containers will draw moisture out of the compost and so will wooden ones. Glazed terracotta, painted wood, fibreglass and plastic containers will not, so these are materials to use if watering is an issue; moreover the fibreglass and plastic ones are lightweight and so are good for moving around and for roof gardens. Self-watering plastic containers made by Stewart will offer further help, as they have a reservoir at the base of the container which can be fed directly by means of a tube. They still need to be watered, but this arrangement will certainly reduce the need for a daily top-up.

To help prevent moisture loss through either the unglazed terracotta or wooden containers, line with black plastic; an ordinary bin liner will be fine or an empty compost bag. If you put the plastic on the floor of the container, be sure to make adequate drainage holes to coincide with those below. This plastic liner will help to keep the container dry which in the case of terracotta will help to prevent frost damage, and in the case of wood will help to prevent wood rot.

grubs will eat the roots of fuchsias, heuchera, primulas, succulents and hostas to name but a few of their favourites, and also the tubers of begonias. They prefer soft multi-purpose compost to a gritty loam-based one, so a gritty compost and gritty mulch might help. Hunt for them at night as they move around in the dark, or look beneath the base of a container where they will hide in the daytime. A twice-yearly application of biological controlling nematodes should zap them, or use a special systemic insecticide. The red lily beetle (*Lilioceris lilii*) will find its way to spring fritillarias and summer flowering lilies and cause devastation both in its adult stage and as the grubs emerge later in summer. Keep alert for them and remove by hand; and if you find one, then look for another, as they rarely feast alone. The best time to look is when the sun is on the plant. Again a special systemic insecticide is available, but please use with caution so as not to endanger other beneficial insects. Grey sawfly (*Phymatocera aterrima*) caterpillars are a menace on Solomon's seal plants; they will not destroy the plant but they certainly render it unattractive. Fortunately they seem to appear once the main flowering display is over and do not affect the plant's ability to flower the following year. Pick them off by hand as soon as you first see them, hunting all over. Alternatively, try a special systemic insecticide.

ABOVE: **Red lily beetle larvae are hidden under a blanket of their own black excrement; when the grubs emerge in late summer they then proceed to eat the lily leaves.**

BOTTOM LEFT: **Solomon's seal sawfly caterpillars attack the foliage in early summer.**

BOTTOM RIGHT: **Vine weevil grubs like to munch through begonia tubers and the roots of many container plants, especially in late summer and early autumn.**

2 BEDDING AND SUCCULENTS

Bedding plants have long been the mainstay of container gardening, used for a temporary display and changed with the seasons. Traditionally, most gardeners change their pots twice a year, often discarding the plants and starting afresh each season. This allows the nurserymen to do all the early work, giving the gardener the pleasure of choosing, planting, caring for and then enjoying the show.

Many of the plants can easily be seed-raised, however, so this can all be part of the container gardener's remit, and if you have a greenhouse, many of the summer flowering plants can be overwintered and enjoyed for a second and often third year. A great deal of flexibility is involved; just find a working pattern that suits you best.

For an easy long-lasting display then succulents spring to mind. They offer variety of form and foliage colour, some flowers, and as well as tender varieties for summer there are hardy succulents which are evergreen and can stay outdoors.

BEDDING PLANTS

Since bedding plants bloom mainly in summer, the autumn, winter and spring period for pots and baskets is often considered secondary to the main summer season, so much so that lots of people don't bother to make any effort. Worse still, they leave their summer bedding containers still in position, full of dead plants. It will be eight months before the summer season colour begins

again, which is a long period of missed opportunity because this autumn to spring period offers such a wealth of wonderful planting combinations.

Autumn, Winter and Spring

The autumn, winter and spring displays are planted mainly in the early autumn. All the plants have to be hardy to cope with the frost and snow, but strong winds can bring added chill and desiccation of the leaves, so make sure the pots are in a sheltered place. Also be aware that in winter the sun will be low in the sky, and the areas receiving full sun will be much more limited than during the summer.

Favourites amongst container bedding plants are violas, pansies, bellis daisies, primroses, polyanthus, primulas, forget-me-nots and wallflowers. Best in a sunny spot they will also cope with partial shade. These are all pretty, either on their own or mixed with each other. Add ivy and bulbs to the combination, and you have a multitude of options for containers from autumn right through to spring. Forget-me-nots and wallflowers will not flower until spring, but most of the other bedding plants might well have some flowers in the autumn, albeit their major display will be in spring.

Primulas and polyanthus both make an important contribution to the spring patio, offering a range of flower colours; the primulas flower slightly earlier with one bloom to a stem while the polyanthus are multi-flowered. Both are scented and both can be kept in their containers and enjoyed another year. But take care to keep them moist, so move the container into a shady spot for summer. They always look lovely with dwarf early

OPPOSITE: **Pansies are among the most popular of all bedding plants; they are available in a wide variety of colours, and those with the bee line markings offer added interest.**

daffodils such as *Narcissus* 'Tete-a-Tete', 'Jack Snipe' and 'Jetfire'.

The double daisy *Bellis perennis* is another container bedding plant often used with the primrose family. It is available in white, pink and red. It is a hardy biennial sown in summer, planted out in autumn and flowers the following spring. Two sizes of daisies can be used. The smaller pincushion type with ball-shaped flowers is the older bedding variety and is particularly pretty and neat. The larger one is a more recent introduction. It is often described as 'giant-flowered' or 'monstrous', though in truth it will only grow to about 15–20cm. Quite often its petals have tips a different colour, creating a quill effect. Either way, the double daisy is one of those plants which is definitely worth growing. It has an old world charm, and for a simple cottage garden look might be grown in small terracotta pots or wicker baskets, either on its own or with other bedding plants such as violas and polyanthus, and also with bulbs. For a late spring partnership, try growing it with herbs. The flowers are edible and will look quite at home along with parsley, thymes and chives.

One of the 'must grow' plants for spring pots and baskets is violas, which are now available in white, cream, yellows, pale and dark blue and orange, with lots of bicolours and picotee edges. Some of the faces have wonderful patterned lines to attract the bees. Sweetly scented, they really are one of the prettiest of all flower groups, perfect in small or medium containers. They are compact in growth, reaching about 15cm high and wide, although the newer trailing varieties will fall to about 40cm, making them ideal for hanging baskets and wall pots. Add contrasting foliage such as ivy *Hedera helix* in either its green or

TOP: **Pretty pink primulas look beautiful with the giant-flowered *Bellis perennis* in this small painted basket.**

BOTTOM: **Separate pots of pompon and giant daisies take the eye along the top of the wall, giving weeks of colour from mid to late spring and into early summer.**

Bees love blue flowers, and in this blue glazed pot these pansies are definitely a great choice.

Pale blue pansies make an excellent interplanting for tall tulips such as mid season *Tulipa* 'Negrita' and pretty pink *T.* 'Angelique' which matures two weeks later.

variegated form, golden feverfew *Tanacetum parthenium* 'Aureum' or silver-leaved cineraria *Senecio cineraria* 'Silver Dust' with its finely divided silvery white foliage, or in a larger pot you might have all three. For extra interest think about planting some dwarf daffodils such as *Narcissus* 'Topolino', 'Hawera', or 'Bellsong' and dwarf mid to late flowering tulips such as *Tulipa* 'Peach Blossom', 'Bakeri Lilac Wonder', 'Honky Tonk' or 'Lady Jane'. Violas can also be used as an underplanting to a shrub or standard tree in a wooden half barrel or large terracotta pot. Try them as a seasonal bedding scheme beneath a mahonia, rosemary, bay or holly. Violas are available to buy in bedding packs in both the autumn and spring.

Deservedly popular, pansies are larger in growth than violas and may reach 20cm or more in height and width. Their faces will be double the size, so any with pretty bee lines or wavy edges to their petals will be even more distinctive than their smaller cousins. However, unless the winter is particularly mild, they are usually rather later to flower than violas, making them a better companion for mid to late spring bulbs than any winter or early spring types. They make a perfect interplanting for tall late tulips and with so many colours of both to choose from, every year you can have a different combination. Pale blue pansies are excellent with either mid season beetroot-coloured *Tulipa* 'Negrita' or the glorious late season pale pink *Tulipa* 'Angelique'. This scheme gives many weeks of colour. Yellow pansies and bright red *Tulipa* 'Apeldoorn' also make a good partnership, and an arresting one. Subtle or explosive, the opportunities are endless.

Scented golden wallflowers give a great performance in spring, planted on their own or with forget-me-nots or late flowering tulips.

Forget-me-nots *Myosotis sylvatica* also make an excellent inter-planting for any late-flowering tulips. They are biennial, planted in autumn pots to flower towards the middle and end of spring. They are another cottage garden favourite, well known for their dainty light blue flowers which make such a valuable contrast to any colour tulip. White and pink forget-me-nots are also available to grow from seed or to be purchased as plants in the autumn. They like well-drained soil and often self-seed happily in the right conditions. If they seed in the garden, don't be afraid to move them into your autumn containers ready for the spring show.

Wallflowers *Cheiranthus cheiri* are another standby for spring containers. They too are biennial, sown the previous summer, planted in the containers in the autumn and flowering from mid spring onwards. Pinch out the growing tips when first planting and space about 30cm apart or say five or six to a medium sized pot. You might lose one or two over the winter months, so be generous on first planting. They will not look attractive during the winter, but in the spring they suddenly put on growth and burst into flower lasting for many weeks. Here too, they are good planted with late flowering tulips or with forget-me-nots. There is a wide choice of colour including deep orange, yellow, gold, red and purple. They are often very sweetly scented which is a huge bonus as you can pick a few flowers for the home and let them perfume a room. Bedding wallflowers are grown as biennials and then discarded.

To make container gardening even easier, violas, pansies, primulas, polyanthus and bellis daisies are all available to buy in the spring as well as the autumn. So too are pots of spring bulbs in

TOP LEFT: *Viola* 'Sorbet Orange Duet' make a pretty picture from autumn to early summer, here on a step ladder along with pots of flowering variegated London pride *Saxifraga x urbium* 'Aureopunctata'.

TOP RIGHT: Golden feverfew *Tanacetum parthenium* 'Aureum' sits well with all violas; dwarf bulbs would make good additions.

growth; choice is more limited and in the case of the bulbs they will work out more expensive, but you can achieve excellent results this way. It means that if you have just moved home and are desperate for some colour, or you simply missed the autumn planting slot or the winter was very severe, you have a second chance to enjoy instant spring colour in your pots and baskets.

Summer Containers

Summer offers huge possibilities for containers in a myriad of places around the home and garden. This is the time to deck out the terrace with a riot of colour, create a great display around your doorway, on the balcony, on the windowsills, walls, and tables. Whether in sun, partial shade or full shade, there are possibilities everywhere.

Timing is crucial. All the plants discussed in this summer section will be frost sensitive and must only be placed outside after all threat of frost has passed. This varies a little from year to year and certainly according to locality whether it is rural or urban, north or south; generally the watershed is end of spring to early summer but local conditions will always make a big difference. A south-facing windowsill will always be more sheltered and warmer than a north-facing porch. The easy option is to buy your plants in early summer; then you bear no risk of frost damage. Moreover, if you have planted pots with hardy daisies, violas, pansies and wallflowers as described in the previous section then you will not have missed out at all as they will still be in flower. You might also be enjoying hardy herbaceous flowering plants at this time of year such as Solomon's seal, and *Dicentra spectablis*.

If you have a greenhouse, you can plant up the summer containers in mid to late spring and allow them to be growing on, ready for the time

Lobelia is one of the mainstays of the summer patio, available in many shades of blue, and with purple, rose and white as well.

when the frosts cease. Once established, many people put the pots outside in late spring, bringing them into the shelter of the greenhouse in the evening when the temperatures might drop to near freezing or below. This method, called 'hardening off', helps the plants to adjust gradually to the lower outside temperatures. This is when keen containers gardeners are at their busiest – taking care of the watering, watching the weather forecast and deciding whether to leave the plants outside or not.

For those without a greenhouse, but with a sunny inside window sill, then it is possible to start off some of these plants from seed yourself and then once they have been pricked out and become established it is time to pot them up into their summer containers outside. The weather issues will just be as crucial: beware frost.

Many of the plants used in summer bedding schemes for containers are grown each year from seed. Two of the most common are lobelia and busy Lizzie *Impatiens wallerana*. Both offer a wide range of colour opportunities and are tolerant of shade and partial shade, hence their deserved popularity. Full sun can cause stress in high summer so best to avoid, if possible, or at least pay close attention to watering in this situation. Lobelia comes in a range of light and dark blue, purple, rose and white with the option of compact or trailing varieties. Busy Lizzies are available in over twenty shades of pink, salmon, red, mauve and white self colour and bicolour single flowers; as well rosebud doubles. There is even a variegated double called 'Fiesta Olé Peppermint'. So the combinations of lobelia and busy Lizzies are multitudinous. You could spend a lifetime of container gardening using the same two plants but in different colour combinations. They could be all white; salmon and white; red white and blue; or pale pink and pale blue, to name just a few. Matching hanging baskets and pots would tie the whole patio together.

Salmon pink busy Lizzies look good and safe with pale or dark blue lobelia.

Double pink variegated busy Lizzies look edgy with rose coloured lobelia.

Building on this key relationship, there is another plant which will add height and body to the scheme – the fuchsia. Fuchsias are ideal, loving the same kind of conditions of shade or partial shade and offering excellent colour coordination. There are many different ones to try, but for a spot with four to six hours of sun try the Triphylla type with its clusters of long tubular red-orange flowers; then you will have a show stopping combination. Two cultivars are 'Thalia' and 'Coralle'. Either will grow both about one metre tall and wide, so eventually cover the width of any pot in which they are planted. Their strong flower colouring adapts well to plain terracotta or glazed pots as seen here with these red and blue coloured containers. You can grow them on their own or mix them with salmon pink busy Lizzies and blue lobelia. Move the pot into a frost free greenhouse during the winter and, although you will lose the underplanting (the lobelia may self seed) the fuchsia will survive and make a glorious show next summer. If you add a begonia at the base, just take the entire pot into the greenhouse, and next spring the begonia and fuchsia will come into growth once more.

Fuchsia 'Coralle' makes a striking picture just on its own.

Fuchsia 'Coralle' also looks good with salmon pink busy Lizzie and lobelia.

Fuchsia 'Coralle' makes a vibrant display planted with an orange begonia.

Fuchsias also make very good hanging basket material, just be sure to choose ones with a drooping or lax habit. Those with semi-double or double flowers will trail lower. There are many to choose from. Lobelia and busy Lizzies are ideal companions here too.

If you want a stunning tall scheme, then consider a half or full standard fuchsia, which has been trained to flower on top of a tall stem either 50cm or 75cm high. Add in the height of the pot, and once the fuchsia has matured, you will have an arrangement which will be close to eye level. This makes the impact so much more powerful. The downside is that any tall planting scheme will act like a sail on windy days, and you need to anchor the plant securely. So first of all choose a sheltered spot. Be certain to retain the support

cane to which the plant is attached, or add another longer one if necessary so that it pushes down securely into the soil, and then retie. Choose a heavy wide-based container in which to plant it. Terracotta or glazed pots are ideal. Add a brick in the base for even more ballast. Always use a soil-based compost which has grit added so that you have a good long-term soil structure. Fuchsias like a moist soil, so regular watering is essential. They also enjoy an evening misting from above and below; this keeps the plant fresh but it also deters some of the insects that thrive on fuchsias, such as red spider mite.

Other suggestions for tall arrangements using quarter, half or full standards are *Solanum ranton-nettii*, heliotrope, abutilons and lantana. They make a beautiful focal point to a patio, or as a pair would look good on either side of a door or entrance gate. The solanum is a deciduous shrub also known as Paraguayan nightshade, it has rich blue scented flowers and like the fuchsia enjoys some shade so busy Lizzies and lobelia can be used as before. Or try another blue carpeting plant called *Sutera cordata* 'Blue Showers', which is a relative newcomer to the container garden plant palette. It is also available with pink flowers although the most popular form is white 'Snowflake'. Smothered in blooms, it makes a versatile option in all its shades and is happy in sun or partial shade.

Heliotrope, abutilons and lantana like full sun, and any plants grown underneath, in association with them, should be sun-loving too. *Lantana camera* is deciduous and is available in several colours including yellow or an interesting orange and pink combination. Its flowers and leaves smell like pineapple. Try sun-loving yellow French marigolds Tagetes or yellow *Argyranthemum frutescens* at the base. For contrast, add pale blue *Convolvulus sabatius* to trail over the rim, but be aware, its flowers close in the evening.

Abutilons have delicate bell-shaped or open bowl-shaped flowers which are often rich reds, orange or yellow. 'Kentish Belle' is a deservedly popular form with small yellow and crimson flowers. Tagetes or convolvulus would both make good bedfellows.

Heliotrope also makes a good standard. It is evergreen and needs a warm, sheltered spot where you can really enjoy the sweet fragrance. For ground cover, choose blue *Convolvulus sabatius* or *Sutera cordata*.

TOP: **This standard fuchsia makes a striking picture in its pink pot with pale blue lobelia as a simple underplanting; the pink** Begonia **'Non-Stop' sitting beside it echoes the fuchsia's colour.**

BOTTOM: Solanum rantonnettii **is a fragrant shrubby plant, here surrounded by** Sutera cordata **'Blue Showers' to soften the rim of the pot.**

Sun-loving *Lantana camera*, trained as a standard plant, is grown here with yellow *Argyranthemum frutescens*, along with pretty blue *Convolvulus sabatius* to trail over the sides of the pot.

Use repetition of plants to make a big impact on the patio. Fuchsia, *Solanum rantonnettii*, heliotrope, lantana and abutilon can each be obtained as smaller shrubs as well as the more expensive standard form. Double up your plants and echo the colour scheme around the patio. The good news is that, with winter protection, the argyranthemum, sutera and convolvulus will live to make an even better display, along with their larger partners, next year.

Pelargonium are another major sun-loving bedding plant which are excellent for containers, long in bloom and capable of surviving for several years if kept in frost-free conditions during the winter. Confusingly their common name is geranium (though not related to *Geranium* or cranesbill). Their flower colours range through many shades of pink, white and red whilst their leaves sometimes have intricate zoning. Most are upright but some, known as the ivy leaved types, are trailing in habit which makes them useful for hanging baskets, window boxes and wall pots. They are a must for containers where there is lots of sun although they will also perform well in partial shade. Conveniently, like succulents, they will tolerate fairly dry conditions, so for the busy gardener they are not as dependent on a daily drink as are lobelia and busy Lizzies.

If you are growing for easy maintenance and high impact just use one pelargonium per pot, with nothing else at all. Where you want an old-fashioned mix of summer colour then you will probably add something like lobelia, petunias or busy Lizzies, but the pelargonium itself will not perform as well as if it is grown on its own.

For simple airy-fairy charm try scented pelargoniums grown in individual pots close to your herbs. Choose several different ones and place them in a sunny sheltered spot where you will often walk past, touch the leaves and enjoy the fragrance of rose, peppermint, nutmeg, lemon, peppermint and chocolate; they are irresistible. But if you like something more showy, then try the regal pelargoniums with their large blooms and ruffled petals. Recent breeding with this group means that the new introductions flower much longer than the older cultivars so popular in the nineteenth century, which tended to give up flowering by mid-summer.

Petunias love the sun and are a popular patio plant with a wide range of colours, from pink to blue to white, either single or double and with a sweet perfume. Again they are available in different sizes with upright, miniature and trailing being commonly on offer, all with different parts to play depending on the look required.

For a truly fantastic partnership in hanging baskets and window boxes try trailing or Petunia Surfinia[PBR] with *Scaevola aemula*. Loving sun, but also happy in partial shade, they are both big growers ,and during the course of the season they

Pelargonium 'Sweet Mimosa' has scented foliage and dainty pink flowers.

Pelargonium 'Black Prince' is an elegant Regal type with joyous rich colouring.

Scaevola aemula 'Blue Wonder' and 'Zig Zag' are both planted in this 35cm diameter lined wicker basket along with *Petunia* 'Surfinia Hot Red' (PBR) and 'Surfinia Sky Blue' (PBR); the result is a massive display measuring 1.2m tall and across.

will create a 1.2m spectacle in both width and depth. This combination is clever because just as the petunia will fall straight down like a curtain, the scaevola will grow out like a candelabra arching back through the petunia trails with its pretty fan-shaped flowers. *Scaevola* 'Zig Zag' has a white stripe, while 'Blue Wonder' is an intense blue. Both make super hanging basket material with the trailing petunias whether red, pink, blue or white, in either full sun or partial shade. Don't bother with any side planting. Also, there's no need to add any other plants in the top. Just let these two plants do all the talking.

In recent years *Scaevola aemula* has made a big impact on the container gardening front, largely because the plant simply goes on flowering better and better as the summer progresses. It can be grown from seed or cuttings and will overwinter in a greenhouse. It makes a very good companion to begonias, which also get better and better as summer turns to autumn. If you have a greenhouse, the pot can simply be overwintered and brought out again the following spring.

Another winning combination but on a much smaller scale is diascia and brachyscome. Choose *Diascia barberae* 'Blackthorn Apricot' or 'Ruby Field', the first with apricot, the second with deep salmon flowers with a height of 20cm and spread

ABOVE: Rich blue *Scaevola aemula* 'Blue Wonder' makes a lively partner for this yellow non-stop begonia, an ever more impressive display as summer turns to autumn.

A sumptuous summer basket with two salmon pink *Diascia* 'Little Drifter', two *Nemesia* 'Golden Eye' and two blue Swan River daisies *Brachyscome* in a lined wicker basket 38cm × 27cm × 20cm deep.

of 30cm. *D.* 'Little Drifter' is a slightly smaller form at 15cm high and wide. Then add blue Swan river daisy *Brachyscome iberidifolia* which will grow to around 30cm or more. The result is a delicate airy arrangement which is delightful in pots and hanging baskets but especially lovely in cottage-style baskets with a handle. Depending on the size of the basket you may plant one brachycome in the middle with a diascia on either side. Or if the basket is bigger, then alternate three diascias and three brachyscome with two at each end and two beneath the handle.

The diascia will benefit from regular deadheading throughout the summer, but eventually by early autumn the brachyscome may have become dominant. To retain the balance and extend the flowering season well into the autumn try a severe haircut in early August. Cut all the top growth off, leaving just 3–5cm of growth. Water well and apply a liquid feed, and by the end of the month lots of new growth will be made, and soon flowering will begin again all with renewed vigour. As autumn approaches this will look wonderfully fresh and colourful, and if night-time frosts threaten just move the basket inside for the night or put in a greenhouse. It will continue to bloom for weeks and depending on the weather you may be enjoying it until nearly Christmas.

Nemesia is another plant that can be added to this mix in either its pink, white, lavender or blue forms. It has the same delicate look and will mound well with the brachyscome and diascia. It will also respond very well to the early August haircut. Treat all three plants as short-lived, and start again next year with cuttings taken in the previous summer or new plants from the garden centre.

Growing Container Plants from Seed

You can buy a wide choice of young plants in late spring and early summer from many different outlets, but if you grow from seed then you will have many more possibilities as to flower colour and foliage. Two of the easiest plants to try, without the need of a greenhouse, are sweet peas and nasturtiums.

Sweet peas *Lathyrus odoratus* come in a wonderful range of colours, and many though not all have a super fragrance; being a hardy annual none of them need the protection of a greenhouse. There are over 1,000 cultivars to choose from including many with frilly petals, self-colours, bi-colours, some wonderfully scented, some not (always check on the packet or in the seed catalogue). You can often buy them as mixed packets so you can grow lots of colours together. Using a multi-purpose compost, you can sow them into root trainers or direct in the pots or tubs where you want them to grow. Germination will take approximately ten days (in a greenhouse) or more (outside). Beware mice and slugs.

Choose a sunny spot to grow them during the summer months. Always use canes or trellis for support. Some growers like to sow in the autumn to get earlier blooms and stronger plants, but sowing in mid to late spring is fine for most people. Pinch out the growing tips of the young plants when they are about 10cm high which will encourage lateral shoots. With a regular liquid feed of a balanced fertilizer, such as a tomato feed, they will flower well in the height of summer and

Sweet peas are easy to sow and grow in containers on the balcony or patio, where they can be picked for a posy indoors.

you can pick the blooms for your home to your heart's content. The more you pick the better as they will continue to flower that way; if they are allowed to form seed heads, they will soon give up flowering. One of the drawbacks to sweet peas is greenfly. Another is the black pollen beetle which particularly love light blue flowers; there is no cure, simply choose the darker colours.

Tropaeolum majus, known more commonly as nasturtium, makes another excellent choice for easy seed sowing. It offers exciting colour combinations as well as choice of foliage – some dark green as in 'Cobra', some mottled with cream as in 'Alaska'. Some will climb 1.2m, others will trail 75cm, some are compact. Your choice will depend on where you want to grow them. Sown in mid spring, they will need protection from frost, but if you leave sowing until late spring,

they can be sown direct into their outdoor containers and will only take two weeks to germinate. They can easily be grown on their own and make a lovely idea for a chimney pot where they will trail around the sides. Or mix them with begonias in a hanging basket or pot. Pale yellow and red 'Strawberries and Cream' would be ideal with yellow or red trailing or non-stop begonias. The nasturtium will come into flower before the begonia really takes off, providing the early and mid summer colour, leaving the begonia to take over until the autumn frosts. Alternatively grow them in your raised vegetable beds to trail around the sides. Buds, flowers, young leaves and semi-ripe seeds can all be eaten in salads and omelettes. Choose a site in full sun or partial shade. Blackfly may be a problem – the healthier the plant the less likely it will be affected. But if an infestation does occur, act quickly and just remove the affected leaves or growing tips.

HOUSE PLANTS OUTDOORS

Many house plants will thank you for a summer vacation outside in the fresh air. Two favourites are the spider plant *Chlorophytum comosum* 'Variegatum' and *Tradescantia zebrine* also known as wandering Jew. They will both enjoy light shade, will thrive in the great outdoors and come back into the house in the autumn. The spider plant will eventually mature to have little white flowers on the end of long stalks which then produce a profusion of hanging plantlets. In time these can be taken off to form new plants, but in the meantime you will enjoy an impressive display of around 75–90cm drop, which makes a good subject for a wall pot or hanging basket. The tradescantia has small blue flowers, but it is the foliage which is the more impressive with strong stripes on the top of the leaves and a rich purple below, making a sumptuous mound useful for a wall pot or hanging basket display.

SUCCULENTS

Easy to grow from seed, nasturtiums will trail over troughs, tumble out of baskets and generally add cheer wherever they appear.

If you want an easy care summer patio display then consider succulents. When using succulents,

Houseplants spidery *Chlorophytum comosum* 'Variegatum' and purple tinged *Tradescantia zebrine* will enjoy partial shade on the summer patio.

moist. Extra water will not harm the plants so long as the compost has good drainage, so ensure this by adding one-third extra grit at the time of planting.

One of the most popular groups of tender succulent come from the echeveria family, which is native to the higher regions of Mexico and the surrounding area. They enjoy full sun but will tolerate shade for part of the day. They vary in size and leaf colour and shape, but generally they form low-growing rosettes which remain neat all year round. They flower at various times from early to late summer on long flower spikes, and their flower colour is either yellow or a warm salmon pink. Many produce offsets around the mother plant so that a dense colony can form in

Echeverias with their tight rosettes of small fleshy leaves are good as single specimens in small pots. *E. imbricata* (top left), *E. elegans* (bottom left) and *E.* 'Violet Queen' (right) make an interesting table arrangement, each showing subtle variations.

the main point to consider is that the tender succulents can only live outdoors for the summer, so during the autumn, winter and spring months they must be kept either indoors on a light windowsill or in a frost-free greenhouse. The hardy varieties can remain outside all year round.

Tender Succulents

Succulents are strong in form and offer an exciting range of foliage colour. Moreover some have stunning flowers. They will all enjoy full sun and need very little extra care. Natural rainfall will provide sufficient moisture for the plants most of the time, although it is always good practice to check that the compost remains at least barely

due course. These are easily separated and can be planted up to form new displays. *Echeveria elegans* is one of the most common forming small tight plump rosettes, whilst *E. imbricata* is rather larger and soon forms a sizeable display 30cm or more across, with much flatter leaves. The minutiae of succulent leaf colour and form is addictive, and a group together make a simple but effective arrangement for a patio table, window sill or series of wall pots.

If you like powdery grey pink foliage then consider *Echeveria* 'Perle von Nurnberg'; the rosettes reach around 15cm wide, and it flowers well. Or try a slightly larger form reaching around 20cm across called *E.* 'Violet Queen', with dense rosettes of silver grey which curl up slightly and take on a purple hue at the tips in autumn. Larger still and even more attractive is *E.* 'Afterglow'; it forms a rosette of around 30cm or more wide with orange red flowers, and has lavender grey leaves with glowing pink edges. For full effect, position it so that you can see it with the warm evening light behind it. Flower spikes normally emerge from below the lower leaves; if they develop as a terminal inflorescence then they are best removed or else further growth on that rosette may be aborted.

There are many other succulents to choose from including the agave family of which *Agave americana* 'Variegata' is one of the most popular. It lives many years and forms younger plants around the base; these should eventually be removed and planted up separately to avoid breaking the pot as the roots are very strong. It rarely blooms, but the distinctive leaf structure more than makes up for any absence of flowers. It will reach up to 75cm high and wide within a few

TOP: *Echeveria* 'Afterglow' makes a stunning specimen plant for the summer patio table and would grace any conservatory table through the winter months. *Photo: Vanessa Kay*

BELOW: All echeverias have long showy spikes of mainly orange, salmon or yellow flowers which last for many weeks; *Echeveria* 'Afterglow' is a prime example. *Photo: Vanessa Kay*

Succulents look good alongside begonias and grasses, especially where they have beautiful foliage colour and form such as *Agave americana* 'Variegata' (centre) and *Echeveria* 'Gypsy' with frilly pink edges (right of centre) as well as wavy *E. runyonii* 'Topsy Turvey' (centre right).

is popular for patio displays. It develops a trunk, often branching to around 1m high, and then on mature plants in spring it has clusters of tall yellow flowers. It will tolerate moist or dry conditions. Propagation is easy. Remove a side branch, allow 24 hours for it to form a callus, then insert into a gritty mix of barely damp compost.

The black aeonium is super planted just on its own, or try it with a skirt of slightly pointed *Sedum morganianum* or rounded *Sedum burrito*, both often grown as trailing house plants. These sedums also make excellent specimens for summer outdoor hanging baskets along with larger echeverias such as *E*. 'Imbicata'. These three plants will be happy to live in light conditions indoors during the winter as well as a frost-free greenhouse.

Black *Aeonium arboreum* var. *atropurpureum* 'Schwarzkof' makes a distinctive display along with various echeveria including tall *E*. 'Paul Bunyon' with its lumpy leaves. The glass daisies make a playful addition, mimicking the form of the open rosettes of the aeoniums whilst their colour echoes the backdrop of the Mondrian style wall. *Photo: Vanessa Kay*

years and looks very good as a single specimen plant on its own. It will also make a striking centrepiece for a mixed arrangement alongside begonias and grasses, all of which are easy to look after without the need for constant watering. There are endless associations which would look attractive, but it always helps with the younger agaves to raise them up to a level where they can be more fully enjoyed. They will look good on a metal or wooden table, on top of a low wall, or as here staged on top of two rusty metal cubes.

Aeonium arboreum comes from the Canary Islands and is normally green, but it is the black form *A.a.* var. *atropurpureum* 'Schwarzkof' which

This is easy container gardening: the herb pot has been planted with these same sempervivums and *Sedum spathulifolium* 'Cape Blanco' for over ten years.

Hardy Succulents

The succulents mentioned here are evergreen so are useful as a display all year round. The ones most often grown in containers are those from the sempervivum family, commonly known as house-leeks. They are native to the alpine regions of Europe and are thoroughly hardy, being used to several inches of snow cover during the winter. As long as they have good drainage with 25–50 per cent sharp grit added to the compost and an open sunny position, then they are very easy to look after. A top dressing of grit between plants also helps the winter wet problem where snow is not a long-term winter occurrence. They are tolerant of wind and only need occasional attention.

Their flowers are not as showy as the eche-verias mentioned earlier but they are welcome nevertheless. Once they have finished flowering, that rosette will die and is best removed. Add a little new compost, so that new growth can cover the gap.

They are often grown in shallow alpine troughs where they will eventually form tight rosettes around the edge of the planter. The four-tiered pot opposite has been planted out for over fifteen years with a selection of sempervivum around the bottom tier, including the cobweb houseleek *Sempervivum arachnoideum* with its tight green rosettes covered with pale silvery fibres like a spider's web. The stonecrop *Sedum spathulifolium* 'Cape Blanco' with its fleshy silvery leaves has been planted in the top – a hardy mat-forming stone crop from the Pacific Northwest of the USA which is really good in shallow containers.

Two golden stonecrops, this time from Europe, are *Sedum acre* 'Aureum' and *Sedum rupestre* 'Angelina'. Both are very useful to provide an almost flat carpet of greenery at soil level beneath a topiaried box or yew, or standard holly. Both are evergreen, and particularly welcome in winter.

For simple ideas which cost virtually nothing, try 'micro gardening' with sempervivums planted in eggshells. Sempervivums are easy to propagate. Gently pull off the rosettes from established plants, or buy plants with several rosettes already growing and propagate from those. The rosettes normally pull away with a little bit of root showing at the base. You can mix and match or just plant different ones as you wish; some of the leaves will be green, some have copper or bronze flushes, some have red tips. For fun containers, buy some large eggs, and hard boil them. Carefully take off the lids and remove the contents. Then with a pin make a hole at the base for drainage. Add a few teaspoons of compost, a little grit and plant your offsets. Water gently and then leave outside to grow. Plastic decorated Easter eggs also work if you can remove the top and remember to make a drainage hole at the base. Show them off on a tiered egg stand or a metal cupcake stand. If using real eggshells, after six months or so you might have to replant.

3 FRUIT, VEGETABLES AND HERBS

Container gardening can produce a rich harvest of delicious foods – a wide range of fruits, vegetables, herbs and even edible flowers. Treat your pots and baskets as your larder; keep them close to your kitchen door where you can pick and pluck to your heart's delight.

Your very own kitchen garden is such a valuable asset, on however small or large a scale. Just one basket of tomatoes will give you pleasure; add some basil plants and you have the makings of a very tasty meal. Plant some salad leaves in a window box, some French beans in a planter, grow courgettes and herbs and then you have the basis of many meals. No air miles here – everything will taste fresh, juicy and delicious.

FRUIT

Apples

Ordinary apple trees grow too large for normal containers, so you should always consider a dwarf variety. Pear trees are occasionally offered as dwarfs, but there is much more choice with apples. The key to choosing a suitable apple is to look at the rootstock on which the tree is grafted. It is this feature which will determine how tall the tree will eventually grow. For container purposes purchase a tree that is grafted onto P-22 (1.5–2m), M-9 (1.6m) or M-27 (1.9m) rootstock. Look at the label on the tree for this information. If purchasing online or through a catalogue, search out this important detail.

OPPOSITE: **Tomatoes, basil and chillis make a sumptuous top tier to this A-frame vegetable planter, with watercress, carrots and chard below.**

The M-27 size is one of the most popular sizes, but your choice may depend on the nursery from which it is grown and also the variety. The M-27 rootstock will give you a tree which will grow to approximately 1.9m in ten years. This size of tree means that you can see the blossom and fruit at eye level, giving maximum enjoyment and making the fruit easy to harvest.

Next you need to consider whether the apple you choose needs another apple to pollinate it or whether it is self-fertile, meaning that it does not need another apple nearby with which to cross-pollinate. In any case it is usually preferable to grow at least two apple trees as the fruit harvest that they produce will be more prolific and a better quality if pollinated by another apple tree.

Plant varieties that will bloom around the same time; otherwise the apples will not be able to pollinate one another. There are five pollination groups, but luckily if you choose an apple from say Pollination Group 3 it will also be pollinated from a tree in Group 2 and 4, as well as 3, which makes it easier. The label will often indicate which other varieties make good cross-pollinators. Urban and rural gardens are often full of apple trees so with luck, somewhere nearby, there will usually be the perfect partner.

When you choose your tree think about whether you want a dessert or cooking apple. If the former do you like one that turns rosy red, is deliciously flavoured, crunchy, and keeps well? Maybe you would like bright red, juicy *Malus* 'Discovery' which ripens in mid August. The fruits will last a few weeks but they are best eaten straight from the tree. For one that ripens in early October, choose 'Red Falstaff'. It is both aromatic and juicy, self-fertile, a good pollinator and one of the best of all garden apples. It keeps until March.

These both belong to Pollination Group 3. *Malus* 'Bramley' AGM is the most popular cooking apple ripening in October. Crisp and firm it is still the most popular of its type. It falls into Group 3 and unusually needs two pollinators. The apples are large and heavy, and for container growing the 'Bramley Clone 20' is probably the best choice as it has 20 per cent less vigour than its parent.

If you buy in a garden centre then the trees will usually be grown in containers. Avoid any with disease on the leaves. When you come to plant, if the roots are tightly bound, tease some of them

Apple *Malus* 'Discovery' is growing on an M-27 rootstock. You can plant herbs such as chives, and sage around the base of the tree, or try low growing spring bulbs , to be followed by a few pots of geraniums or busy Lizzies, simply placing them on top of the compost, and removing them in the autumn to allow the bulbs to perform again.

out so that early new growth is easily made. If you buy in the late autumn/winter months from a catalogue you may well find that the plants are sent with bare roots – that is to say with no soil around them. This is normal practice suited to the time of year when they are dormant. In either case, look for a young tree that is one to three years old, as these tend to establish best.

A sunny, sheltered site is needed. Choose a medium-to-large container, ideally one that is flat bottomed, heavy and stable. Eventually, as you move the tree on into an ever larger container, a large wooden half barrel can be used. In any event make sure the drainage holes are adequate and drill them if necessary. You want your tree to last several years in its new home (whether terracotta or wood), so to maximize its longevity line the sides and base of your container with a plastic bin liner or the plastic from a sack of soil. This will prevent moisture loss through evaporation, and in the case of a wooden barrel will prevent the onset of rot where moist soil continually hits the wood, which most frequently occurs at the base of the barrel.

Cover the base with 5cm or more of drainage material and then a soil-based gritty compost such as John Innes No 3 to fill the barrel. Soak the tree, and then place in the container so that the graft union (the bulging point near the bottom of the trunk where the tree was grafted onto its rootstock) is level with the rim of the pot or barrel. Add more compost until the finished height of the compost is 2.5–5cm below the rim; firm down the compost and water well.

Stake the tree to help support it in its early years, so that it grows upright. Your tree will need less water in its dormant period, so just ensure compost is moist to the touch. Although it is hardy, never water in frosty weather. From spring onwards as the blossoms and leaves emerge its water needs will increase. Check weekly. In hot weather you may need to water daily. It is best to feed with a general slow-release fertilizer in late winter, and then fortnightly with a liquid feed throughout the growing period.

Pruning is generally performed in mid winter when the branches are bare, the plant is dormant, and the structure can be easily seen. The aim is to have a clean structure where each branch can benefit from maximum sunlight. The main trunk should have three or four branches pointing out to the sides with each side branch about 15cm up or down the trunk from the other side branches. Remove any dead or damaged branches and also any branches that are pointing inwards or that cross (or will eventually cross) another branch.

Lemons

The idea of growing an orange or lemon or lime tree might appeal to you and these plants often become available to use around Christmas or Easter time. Of them all, the lemon tree is probably the most rewarding, especially if you choose one which is 'everbearing', i.e. continually fruiting such as *Citrus Limon* 'Four Seasons'. It will flower three or four times a year, fruiting thereafter in succession with flowers and fruit occurring concurrently. A compact plant, the leaves are glossy and evergreen, the flowers are beautifully fragrant, and the lemons themselves of course are useful in so many ways, both in drinks and food.

Citrus Limon 'Four Seasons' is not difficult to grow in just a small pot. Use a well-drained potting compost such as John Innes No 2 soil with 20 per cent added grit to the mix. Water regularly in summer, but less in winter when the compost needs to be kept just barely moist. *Citrus Limon* 'Four Seasons' is one of the hardiest lemon trees available. It will need a winter minimum of 4°C; this may mean bringing it into a light conservatory or sunroom but you may also be able to keep it in a heated greenhouse outside against the warmth of a south-facing house wall. In the summer months keep it on a sunny sheltered patio. Pot on in late winter and feed with a proprietary citrus food for lemons.

Blueberries

Blueberries *Vaccinium corybosum* are relatively easy to grow in containers, although they will only thrive on acidic soil so ericaceous compost is required at the time of planting. They have a shal-

This lemon tree is continually fruiting and makes a wonderful addition to a warm patio.

low fibrous root system and like to be kept moist in summer. Best to use rain water for irrigation and not tap water which usually contains lime and is thus alkaline. Lack of water will adversely affect the cropping, so will overwatering. A regular check throughout the summer months will help, with extra attention during the fruiting season when the berries are developing and swelling. A mulch of bark on top of the container will help preserve the moisture and prevent weeds growing. Other mulches could include compost, seashells or grit. New shoots will develop, pushing up through the mulch, eventually filling the

It is advisable to net the blueberries well before the fruits begin to ripen or else the crop will be eaten by the birds.

canes are fruiting. Whatever you do, make sure you net them to prevent the birds enjoying them more than you do. It is best to do this well in advance of the berries ripening. Blueberries ripen over several weeks and you will get a succession of fruits. Once they have turned blue, they will be ripe, but if left on the canes for a few days more, the flavour will intensify.

Blueberries grow naturally in dense thickets in North America; often to about 1.2–1.5m high. The leaves colour vividly in autumn. In pots they need pruning during the dormant winter months. For the first three years no major work needs to be done at all, except for tidying up, removing twiggy or dead growth. Thereafter, remove two or three of the oldest canes each season in order to promote more vigorous new shoots which will eventually crop better than the weak ones. Fruiting always occurs on the previous season's growth so you should begin to get a crop in the second year after planting, but harvest will be better still in the fourth season.

Strawberries

Strawberries are another soft fruit suitable for containers. They especially benefit by being raised off the ground so that slugs and snails are kept at bay and the fruits remain dry. They can be grown in wicker hanging baskets, a half barrel or large pot, or even the smaller strawberry pots, although the design of these means that the plants along the bottom often dry out too much. Four strawberry plants can be planted into a 35–40cm diameter hanging basket, and with good feeding and watering each two-year-old plant might produce up to 1½lb of fruit.

Use a good multipurpose compost, with a layer of horticultural grit on top to help retain moisture in the hanging basket and also to keep the leaves and fruit of the strawberry plant dry. Place in a sheltered sunny position. Feed every two weeks once flowering has started using a tomato feed. Water carefully to maintain good moisture levels, but avoid getting the fruit wet. Insert some small canes to support netting over the plants to prevent the birds eating the fruit; if it is merely

containers so it is a good idea to pot on regularly each spring. Position the containers in either full sun or light shade.

Most blueberries are self-fertile and will crop even if you have only one plant, although two plants of different varieties will ensure better pollination with higher yields and bigger berries. 'Bluejay', 'Bluecrop', 'Bluegold' are just three reliable varieties to try which will give a good mid season crop. In addition there are many cultivars to choose from offering slightly earlier, mid season and late season varieties which will also produce slight variations in fruit size and flavour.

Use a slow-release fertilizer at the start of the growing season, and thereafter apply a dilute high potash (tomato) feed at regular intervals while the

draped over they will still be able to peck through the netting. You can choose one of the excellent large red berrying kinds or experiment with the smaller alpine or woodland strawberries either red or white fruiting. The red fruits prefer a sunny position; the white will cope with more shade.

VEGETABLES

Containers of many sorts can be used to grow vegetables from hanging baskets, wall pots, window boxes, straw bales, planters and raised free-standing beds. Moreover, the choice of what to grow is vast. Some can be the staple good performers such as tomatoes, potatoes, French beans, beetroots, carrots and sweetcorn, but there may well be room for experimentation – try some

different varieties such as golden beets or purple carrots, or some less well known vegetables, maybe celeriac and chard. Fortunately, seeds are widely available in supermarkets, garden centres and from mail order catalogues, but it is the latter which may well provide the more unusual varieties. The Seeds of Italy catalogue offers sixteen varieties of courgette which are grown in various regions of Italy and elsewhere, some green, some striped, some golden, some long, some rounded, each with a slightly different flavour. It's this kind of choice which makes gardening so exciting.

But watch out, it will be a rollercoaster ride. Some of your crops will do brilliantly one year, maybe not so well the next, while some will do the opposite. Weather plays such an important role, and it is largely out of our hands. Not only

Planted in late spring, these containers are bulging with tasty crops by late summer and early autumn. (The wooden containers shown here are available from Harrod Horticultural.) Beetroot, tomatoes and chard occupy the ladder shelves to the left. Tomatoes fill the hanging basket. Carrots on top, parsley and basil in the middle, and more tomatoes below occupy the 'book shelves'. One courgette, French beans, celeriac, chard fill the manger. Sweetcorn, French beans, spinach and celeriac are planted in the raised bed. Chillis, parsley and tomatoes grow in the wall pots. Tomatoes, chillies and basil fill the top of the A-frame planter, with carrots, spring onions, chard, spinach, and watercress in the trays down below.

will it affect growth rates and productivity, it will also affect whether we get a swarm of aphids or ladybirds. Be a relaxed gardener and take the rough with the smooth. The good news is that lots of pests will stay away from containers anyway, especially if they are raised off the ground. Take time to choose varieties of vegetables that are disease-resistant; you will need to study the small print on the packets.

So long as you remember three important lessons – to water and feed and pick regularly – you will have lots of tasty fresh juicy food for lunch boxes and suppers without having to carry it home from the supermarket.

Courgettes, sweetcorn, dwarf French beans, runner beans, and tomatoes can be sown outside in late spring directly into the containers outside. To make the most of the growing season, however, it is often a good idea to start them off under the protection of a greenhouse or window

sill and then plant them out after risk of frost has passed. Don't worry though if you feel you have missed the boat, or you simply don't have a greenhouse or sunny windowsill; there will be plenty of young seedlings for sale on the market and in the garden centres throughout late spring. Growing from seed just offers more choice. Lots of people will do both, grow some from seed and then be tempted to buy something different growing as young plants.

Courgettes

Courgettes can be grown singly in large pots or will flourish in free-standing raised beds. They even do well on old straw bales with small holes cut out, say 15cm deep and 20cm across filled with John Innes No 2 soil-based compost. Indeed, cropping this way makes good compact growth. Mildew may make the leaves turn silver, but generally speaking that is unsightly rather than problematic to fruiting. Cropping will continue for several weeks during late summer and each plant should yield a steady harvest, so beware too many plants. For one thing each plant can grow rather large, besides which you may have rather an excess of courgettes. But there are

ABOVE: **Courgette flowers are edible, both female and male. But take the male in preference otherwise your courgette crop will suffer.**

LEFT: **Courgette plants produce a prolific crop; this one has woven its way through several young celeriac plants, which will be harvested much later.**

TOP: **Sweetcorn ripens as the cob swells and falls away from the main stem; at the same time the silk tassels turn from green to brown.**

BELOW: **The young kernels are sweet and milky and best cooked and eaten almost immediately after picking; as soon as the cobs are picked the sugar content converts to starch, with a 25 per cent sugar loss within a day of picking.**

plenty of savoury delicious ways to use them and if you would like a change, why not make a gooey chocolate courgette cake, or the flowers can be battered and fried, or just torn into shreds and added to a creamy pasta.

Sweetcorn

Sweetcorn, also called corn on the cob, is quick to germinate, and planting outside follows a pattern similar to courgettes. But whereas courgettes will take up a good deal of space at soil level, even spreading 60cm across a planter and another 60cm down the side, you might expect sweetcorn to grow over 1.2–1.5m high. So watch out if you want to grow a hanging basket just behind it. Sweetcorn plants need to grow in a close formation as they are wind-pollinated; allow 45–60cm between plants. An initial scattering of bonemeal (one handful per square metre) will aid growth.

Knowing when the cobs on the plant are ripe might seem obvious to those who have grown it before but is a mystery to those who have not. It is ready to pick when the cob is swollen, the tassels on the end turn brown and the cob itself begins to drop to a 45 degree angle from the stem. The normal rule is to pick and cook as fast as you can, to enjoy all the flavour and sweetness. The procedure takes rather longer for the smaller cobs on the popcorn variety 'GL Popcorn' which are harvested, dried and then the kernels removed for cooking and popping in butter (be sure to cover the pan!).

Sweetcorn takes up so little space at soil level that an underplanting of salad and other vegetable crops makes good sense. A raised bed

Dwarf bean 'Bellini' does not need staking and continues to crop for very many weeks, providing succulent tasty beans.

table made by Harrod Horticultural, 40cm deep and 1.2m square, can be home to eight sweetcorn plants interplanted with dwarf French beans and mixed oriental salad leaves. These are of the mustard family but there are many salad packets to choose from. They can be sown direct or brought on in seed trays ready to plant out. The salad leaves may be cropped over many weeks, but young leaves are definitely the most tender, so pick often. After the first few weeks the salad crop can be replaced with celeriac, which is a good move. The beans and sweetcorn crop through mid to late summer and into early autumn, leaving the celeriac to mature until late autumn. Dwarf Bean 'Bellini' from the Kew Urban Garden Range sold by Thompson and Morgan is sturdy, upright, compact, prolific and easy to grow. Picking the beans young is definitely the best option, especially as the more you pick the more are produced.

Runner Beans

Runner beans are also excellent in containers although slightly tricky, as they need good support and will benefit from a large, stable pot or wooden half barrel. Bamboo canes are the normal method of support, either strung together at the top or with the help of a plastic ring into which the tops of the canes can be fitted. Another option, however, is to grow dwarf varieties, which need no supports.

Dwarf Runner Bean 'Pickwick' can be sown direct in mid spring, about 20cm apart in a large trough, but needs to kept in a sheltered porch or greenhouse until all risk of night-time frosts has passed. At only 60cm tall it needs no staking. Keep the container in a sunny spot; if you put it on gravel, there will be little trouble from slugs or snails. The red flowers are a glorious show. The beans should be cropped early since the younger they are picked, the more tender they are to eat and the more prolific will be the crop.

Picking the beans encourages further production of flowers. One of the secrets of good pod production is an ample supply of moisture and it is helped in this case because the Stewart Balconnière container is plastic with a self-watering reservoir at the base. The plastic trough sits within a handsome wooden surround handmade by Henry Richardson. Great attention has been paid to its construction with nylon pads fitted at the base of the feet to prevent water drawing up the legs. Various sizes are offered.

Peas

Peas *Pisum sativum* are another favourite vegetable for summer containers and can get off to an earlier start than courgettes, French and runner beans as they are not susceptible to frost damage. Dwarf pea 'Sugar Snow Green' grows well in hanging baskets. It can be interplanted with mint so that the mint tips can be cropped along with the peas, and when the peas are over, the mint can continue to grow and flower and can remain in the basket for another year before being divided. The peas grow about 30cm high but without supports they tend to flop over the sides of the basket, which is rather attractive. Grown more traditionally in a trough, they benefit from the support of canes or some other pyramid structure. Henry Richardson makes wooden obelisks to fit around the Stewart Balconnière troughs with their self-watering reservoirs. Again, various sizes are available.

TOP: **Dwarf runner bean 'Pickwick' does not need support; it was sown directly into a Balconnière self-watering container around which a wooden trellis planter has been fitted.**

BELOW: **Pea 'Sugar Snow Green' was sown directly into a Balconnière self-watering container around which an obelisk has been fitted; the pods are harvested before the peas swell.**

Root Vegetables

Celeriac *Apium graveolens rapaceum* seeds are usually sown in early or mid spring, and then the young plants can be planted outside in late spring or early summer. 'Monarch' is considered one of the best varieties. The harvest comes in late autumn, as it takes a while for the plants to mature and the root to grow to a reasonable size at around 10–15cm. Plenty of water is needed and as the plants mature, it helps to remove the bottom leaves so that the roots are left more exposed. Celeriac is a member of the celery family and its leaves are hollow. These are sometimes cut and used as straws in Bloody Mary cocktail drinks. The root can be grated in salads, cooked as a vegetable, added to stews or soups. It is certainly versatile and very tasty.

Other root vegetables such as carrots and beetroot can be grown in troughs or window boxes; your choice of seed will depend on the depth of your containers. Last year with a maximum soil depth of only 10cm in the trays for the Harrod Horticultural Ladder Vegetable Garden and the A-frame Vegetable Garden, I chose shallow rooting carrots 'Atlas' and 'Supreme Chantenay Red Cored' to intersow with rows of spring onions. The raised trays and the smell of the onions helped to prevent an attack by the dreaded carrot fly. Another tray was home to beetroot 'Alto F1 Hybrid', which is a cylindrical type where the roots stand proud of the soil. More soil can be added around them if you want to leave them in situ for the autumn. The young leaves and stems can be added to green salads or used in risotto. The beets were tender and smooth, rich in colour, small and ideal for chopping or grating in salads, and for cooking.

For cropping potatoes all sorts of containers exist these days, including special potato barrels where a panel can be removed from the side for easy cropping; these are filled with 80 litres of

Small carrots and spring onions make good companions in window boxes and shallow troughs; they are often grown together as the smell of the onion helps to deter carrot fly.

compost and take five seed potatoes. But good old plastic or metal buckets can be used to great advantage too, as they can for dwarf beans and dwarf peas. A gardening club competition was recently held where thirty members had each been given one seed potato to grow in a 14-litre plastic bucket. The winner weighed in with a harvest of over 7lbs; the previous year it had been over 10lbs! The type of potato was 'Estima', known as a 'second early'. The key to the weighty success was Growmore granules mixed in with the initial compost, a subsequent fortnightly dilute liquid feed of Growmore and a daily watering. Another pointer was the choice of seed potato, with preference for small and firm over medium or large. All participants were just amateurs, but it shows how rewarding vegetables can be. The advantage of using individual buckets, or indeed large plastic pots, is that you can try growing as many varieties as you have space for.

Although the crops might not be as prolific, some 'first early' potato varieties would be worth trying, as they would provide a welcome harvest just seventy-five days after planting. 'Duke of York', 'Epicure' and 'Casablanca' are just three examples. Tasty new potatoes are a great bonus. But really you could spend a lifetime trying different varieties: from the whole range of early or main crops whether they are grown best for salads, baking or boiling; whether you are looking for the smooth or knobbly look; whether you prefer red skins or white skins, and maybe you would like to try red flesh as in 'Highland Burgundy Red' or blue flesh as in 'Congo'. You can also juggle your timing. Some seed specialists even dispatch tubers in mid summer ready for a Christmas harvest, although through the autumn and winter they would need to be grown in the safety of a greenhouse.

Tomatoes, Aubergines, Cucumbers, Chillis and Red Peppers

Lots of summer vegetables can be grown in a sunny position outside as well as inside a greenhouse – tomatoes, aubergines, cucumbers and red peppers all spring to mind.

Sweet cherry tomatoes will happily grow in hanging baskets, window boxes and troughs, whilst the more traditional taller types will need supports so are best grown in special tomato grow bags or troughs with designated support in place from the beginning. These larger varieties need the side shoots (grown in the crotch between stem and a branch) removed in order to concentrate the growing effort on flower production rather than all leaves. The smaller bush varieties producing the cherry tomatoes do not need this action. The choice for both kinds, small and large, is vast; shape, colour and flavour will vary with every variety. Just check on the seed packet for all the details including whether it can be grown outdoors as well as in a greenhouse.

You can have great fun growing tomatoes 'Balconi Red' and 'Balconi Yellow' in both window boxes and hanging baskets, enjoying the yellow fruits just as much as the red ones. Indeed they are great fun to mix in a salad bowl. Another bush variety to recommend is 'Gartenperle' which tumbles with great aplomb and produces a lovely crop of sweet red tomatoes. Grown just outside your kitchen door, they make picking tomatoes even easier!

The general rule with hanging baskets is to plant one tomato plant in a 30cm basket, with two in a larger 40cm basket. Try interplanting basil with tomatoes to help deter whitefly. It certainly provides a delicious crop of fresh herbs for that all important, freshly picked, warm tomato sandwich.

Another idea is to plant aubergines with the small cherry tomatoes (*see* overleaf). A window box, measuring 65cm long, 20cm across and 15cm deep, can grow two aubergines and three 'Balconi Red' tomatoes. Both benefited from a sunny position, a similar watering regime and the regular use of a high potash tomato feed. The combination of lovely lilac flowers followed by rich purple flesh is a sumptuous addition to a trough of either yellow or red tomatoes. The aubergine and tomato combination was kept in the greenhouse for the whole summer and provided a generous crop of both fruits well into the autumn. The aubergines were purchased as

ABOVE: Tomatoes and aubergines are growing together in a medium-sized window box enjoying the extra warmth of the summer greenhouse.

BELOW: Cherry tomatoes and aubergines both crop over many weeks.

growing plants from a market stall and the label did not declare the variety, but another time it would be good to grow aubergine 'Baby Rosanna' F1 Hybrid. It only grows 60cm tall and produces small golf ball sized fruit without the bitterness of some of the large varieties.

Greenhouse cucumbers can be a delicate crop to grow, with various problems arising mainly due to dry atmosphere or lack of water, so outdoor cucumbers are generally easier. One of the accepted rules of growing cucumbers is to pinch out the growing tip after six sets of leaves have been produced. This will encourage the quick growth of side shoots and therefore fruit. Feed the plants with a potash fertilizer once fruiting commences, and keep well watered when the fruits begin to form; feed thereafter at two-week intervals. The taller varieties will need support, so use a wigwam of long bamboo canes tied at the top.

Cucumbers are often grown in containers on the patio, and there are some excellent smaller varieties to try which may bear up to twenty cucumbers on one plant. As with any cucumber, it is important to crop them before they get too mature; that way you will enjoy the flavour more and also encourage further cropping. Cucumber mosaic virus is a common problem, with yellow or green mottling on the leaves. As there are no chemical controls available it is best to choose a resistant cultivar such as cucumber 'Green

BOTTOM LEFT: Cucumber mosaic virus is just starting on the bottom leaves; eventually it will mean distorted growth and possibly bitter fruits. Affected plants are best destroyed. In any case cucumbers should be picked young to encourage cropping, and these are both more than ready for the kitchen.

BOTTOM RIGHT: Peppers benefit from some short canes to hold the plants in place when they are cropping heavily with fruit; even with greenhouse warmth they are a late crop to fully ripen.

Fingers', which is described as a lunchbox variety just 10–12cm long; it can be grown indoors or outdoors and has a smooth skin suitable for eating whole.

Peppers and chillis will grow in sheltered sunny spots on the patio, but they really do like the warmer temperatures of a greenhouse. They are both an easy crop to look after and will fruit prolifically. It is worth growing a couple of pepper plants in a bucket-sized container and enjoying the fruit as they turn from green to red. How many chilli plants do you actually need when so many are produced on a single plant? Not many in the average household, but they can always be dried and used to provide extra zest to cooking in the cold winter months. They are certainly colourful and definitely worth growing. Chilli and red pepper jam is an excellent way of preserving both.

Salad Leaves

Salad crops are a very important part of edible gardening and marvellous for containers. There are so many lettuces available to try, either in mixed packets or as single varieties. They germinate quickly and grow so fast, it's often hard to keep up with them. But if you want to skip the seed sowing part, simply buy some growing young plants from the supermarket or garden centre and plant them out. They will live much longer outside in a proper container than indoors on your kitchen windowsill.

Lettuces aren't the only option, however; there are many other salad leaves to grow as well. Young spinach, young beetroot leaves, young carrot tops, young chard are all delicious and tasty; then as they grow older they can be cooked as a

TOP: **Winter frosts turn the radicchio into a wonderful sculpture, while the tulips bide their time in the compost below.**

BOTTOM: **In mid spring vibrant red *Tulipa* 'Apeldoorn' makes a bold contrast to the dark radicchio leaves.**

In late spring the radicchio puts on a new spurt of growth, with fresh leaves ready for the table.

vegetable. Nasturtiums can also be used; the young leaves, buds, and flowers and even the semi-ripe seeds are all edible, peppery and useful additions to salads and omelettes. They have the great advantage that they will trail over the sides of a container. Another aspect is that they attract blackfly, which tend to build up infestations on succulent new growth. Well, you can either nip off the new growth and so remove the infestation or look upon it as a bonus, especially if you are growing beans nearby. For the aphids would sooner attach themselves to the nasturtium than the beans. In any event, ladybirds will soon be on their way to gobble them all up.

What about the autumn months when nights are colder? Radicchio can be sown from mid spring onwards and used as a salad leaf during the summer, but for full heads it is best to sow in mid summer and let the plants overwinter to enjoy the following year. They are so colourful and make ideal bedding plants to grow along with tulips. In the cold frosty days of winter they look stunning and then from mid to late mid spring onwards they make fresh growth and can be enjoyed in the kitchen. The flowers are edible and have a faint chicory flavour. The distinctive bitter flavour of the leaves intensifies with age.

Herbs and Edible Flowers

Most culinary herbs love the sun and enjoy well-drained conditions. The combination of six hours a day or more of sunshine and lean conditions without too much fertilizer intensifies the oils and in turn the fragrance and flavour of the herbs. Rosemary, mint, sage, thyme, chives, bay and oregano are easy examples of perennial herbs which you can enjoy for years, while basil, parsley, dill and coriander are all grown as annuals and need replacing each summer. There are very many more that can be grown as well. Try them on a patio or preferably just outside the kitchen door – the closer, the better.

Rosemary grows well in window boxes, troughs and pots, although occasionally cold winter winds might do partial damage to the plant. So besides choosing a sunny spot, also choose a sheltered one. Various cultivars are available; most are considered hardy including 'Miss Jessopp's Upright' which in time will reach 1m high. However, some of the shorter ones such as *Rosmarinus officinalis* 'Green Ginger' at only 60cm high are only frost hardy. Some are prostrate in habit which makes them ideal for cascading over a pot or basket but beware several of these are frost hardy as well. If you live in a sheltered urban setting, in the south of the UK, this may give you little cause for concern. Otherwise take additional precautions by incorporating extra grit into your compost so that it is extremely well drained. Drainage is key here. The plants will survive much better if the soil is on the dry side in winter. They definitely dislike winter wet. Alternatively give them greenhouse protection in severe weather. Sprigs of rosemary are useful at

ABOVE: *Mentha suaveolens* 'Variegata' makes especially pretty garnishes. Mint leaves have a marvellous piquancy in spring and should be frequently cropped to encourage tender new growth.

RIGHT: As an evergreen herb rosemary is very rewarding in pots and baskets; both leaves and flowers are useful with savoury and sweet dishes in the kitchen.

any time of year with roast vegetables, roast meats and to flavour crab apple jellies. The aromatic flowers are produced over many weeks in springtime and every one, though small, is a tasty and pretty morsel, excellent with patés.

Mint is available in various forms with descriptive names such as spearmint, eau de cologne, ginger, black peppermint, lemon, lime, even basil mint; all are hardy and easy to look after in a series of pots or in a baskets, the sunnier the site, the better. Keep them separate or maybe plant two young plants together in a 35cm diameter hanging basket, and enjoy them for the first summer. Then they will die down during the winter but will reappear the following spring. It is best to divide the plants at this stage and replant, making up new containers if needed. Try growing some small sprigs of spearmint *Mentha spicata* amongst a basket of mangetout peas seeds. It makes the perfect kitchen container for when the peas are ready to harvest. The variegated form *Mentha suaveolens* 'Variegata', also known as the pineapple mint, is normally the last to go dormant and the

last to appear next spring. Both leaves and flowers are delicious in salads and drinks.

Sage is usually available with grey green or bronze leaves. Sometimes an attractive purple, green and cream tricolor sage is sold, but beware as this is not as hardy as the others. In time, and if conditions are rich, sage can spread to 60cm or so. Grow it in poor conditions with little or no added fertilizer. Enjoy the tasty flowers in late spring/early summer, then lightly prune so that it can keep compact. Like rosemary it is an evergreen perennial and therefore useful to crop at any time of year.

Thyme is such a useful herb for the kitchen and so pretty in containers that it is hard to have enough of it. Fortunately there are many different types to grow, varying in height from the creeping thymes at only 5cm high to others which are bushy and might reach 30cm. Lemon scented thyme *Thymus citriodorus* is a favourite, both in its variegated silver form called 'Silver Posie' and its golden variegated form 'Golden Queen'. But you can also find orange-, caraway- and pine-

Sun-loving *Thymus x citriodourus* 'Silver Posie' (left) and *Thymus citriodorus* (right) are both planted here along with variegated mint, parsley and a young lavender.

scented plants. Some are dark green and rather later to flower such as *Thymus pulegioides* known as the broad leaved thyme. Now all these will produce tasty foliage but please don't forget to harvest the flowers. Use them alongside the leaves with chicken and lamb dishes. They are also wonderful with lots of vegetable preparations including baked mushrooms. After the thymes have finished flowering give them a good pruning to keep the plants compact.

Oregano is another herb which is very easy to grow in pots and baskets. It looks good with a range of other plants and is very useful in the kitchen where it is commonly referred to as marjoram. Most varieties are hardy and love a warm sunny position although the variegated and golden leaf forms prefer some shade at midday, otherwise the leaves will scorch. The beautiful golden leaved form *Origanum vulgare* 'Aureum' is super in pots or window boxes alongside mid to late spring bulbs such as dwarf tulips and daffodils, as its fresh green foliage looks so attractive beside them. It is fairly drought-resistant which makes it a good candidate for the bottom holes of so-called strawberry pots where strawberries and other plants so often struggle. The strawberries much prefer the top tier and look delightful hanging down amongst the herb leaves. Oregano flowers are a favourite source of food for the orange tip butterfly so it makes a wonderful insect plant. The flowers are tasty too and go particularly well with tomato dishes and taste wonderful on pizzas. *Origanum onites* is known as pot marjoram, and *Origanum* x onites is known as French marjoram; they are both hardy. Most origanum reach about 45m high in a large container, although in a smaller window box or strawberry pot the growth will be curtailed.

LEFT: Chives *Allium schoenoprasum* are a good subject for containers close to the house, where the leaves can be quickly snipped and used in the kitchen. Grow them with violas and bellis daisies for an attractive late spring/early summer basket.

RIGHT: Pretty and packed with flavour, individual florets of chive flowers *Allium schoenoprasum* make excellent additions to scrambled egg; they are also good as a topping to baked potatoes.

Chives *Allium schoenoprasum* are common herbs easily grown from seed or easy to find as a small pot of growing herbs. The leaves taste of mild onions and are delicious in salads and egg dishes. In late spring or early summer, the lilac flowerheads appear, each one containing several small florets. They are all edible and so pretty, perfect for Sunday brunch with scrambled egg, or scatter them on baked potatoes. In late summer the garlic chive *Allium tuberosum* flowers; it too has edible flowers and leaves, although here the flowers are small and white. Both are easy plants for small pots and baskets.

Many of the herbs grow well from seed, including dill, parsley, coriander and basil. Coriander and dill, however, have a relatively short summer existence. They soon produce flowers and then

shortly thereafter die; sow a succession of crops to maintain supplies.

It may be described as cheat's gardening, but for those who want to skip the seed sowing stage, simply buy a pot of growing herbs from the supermarket or garden centre and then rather than keeping them in the same very limited punnet or pot, plant them into a bigger pot or basket and they will grow away quite happily. Basil and parsley are excellent candidates for this treatment, as are young 'cut again' lettuces or punnets of watercress. A supermarket pot of sweet basil *Ocimum basilicum* with broad tender leaves or the smaller bushier Greek basil *Ocimum minimum* 'Greek' may contain as many as forty young seedlings. They easily split into several smaller clumps and, being a frost tender annual, will grow on quite happily outside from mid-summer onwards, once the colder nights have passed. Basil makes an excellent companion planting with tomatoes to grow either in pots or hanging baskets. Parsley seedlings can be split in the same way and planted amongst other herbs, but they are hardy and if bought in the early autumn can be planted in winter containers.

You can grow the herbs in separate pots on the patio or you can try your very own herb garden in one container. They lend themselves well to wicker hanging baskets and also lined wicker handled baskets; they just seem so natural and attractive in both. A lined winter herb hanging basket with a 35cm or 40cm diameter could include rosemary for height, thymes and oregano as edgers, with parsley in the centre front. Violas and primroses can be added for colour and cropped as edible flowers, as can the flowers on the other bedfellows as they come into bloom during the spring and summer.

For a summer herb hanging basket, you might use lavender as the centrepiece, with clove-scented dianthus, black violas and pink-flowered thymes around the edge. Golden oregano would look attractive there as well. The thymes and oreganos can be cropped for their leaves, whilst all of them produce really tasty edible flowers. The trick will be to purchase young plants that fit well into the space of the container. This could equally suit a medium to large pot.

ABOVE: **Intended for the kitchen window sill, Greek basil can be bought as seedlings from a supermarket.**

BELOW: **Remove from their pot and carefully divide so that you can plant small clumps of basil between your cherry tomatoes. Chillis are also planted here.**

4 HERBACEOUS PLANTS

Herbaceous plants are often ignored in containers. This is a pity because they are extremely worthwhile whether they are conceived as a sole planting idea or together with other plants such as bulbs, grasses or shrubs. Indeed, in a container, herbaceous plants are often quite transformed. Lifted out of the ground and displayed on their own, the beauty and shape of the plant can really be appreciated for their silhouette, leaf markings, intricate flower shapes, scent, beauty of the seed pod and maybe even their shadow.

Just don't expect every herbaceous container to shout out all year round. This type of gardening is more subtle. Be aware that most herbaceous plants are deciduous, with all their leaves and stems dying down to the rootstock in the autumn and lying dormant throughout the cold winter months only to rise up again the following spring. Some might do the reverse, and die back in summer coming to life again the following autumn. These dormant periods are normal, and it is a time for the gardener to be patient, perhaps making sure that there are other containers to be the eye catchers at that time. The evergreens of course will remain green all year round with new leaves being made generally in the spring.

The brilliant news is that some herbaceous plants live for ten or fifteen years, on their own, in the same pot and for this reason may be regarded as extra useful for those container gardeners who don't want to make too many changes; good choices here include very many

ferns, variegated ground elder and Solomon's seal, which are all described below. The best advice is to concentrate on the general condition of the soil, by keeping the compost moist, removing any weeds and above all keeping the plant regularly fed before and during flowering. If the containers are performing well, be content to leave the plants well alone without disturbing the roots.

Other herbaceous plants might live for two or three years before advice is given to divide or repot the plant into a bigger container; heuchera, hosta, primroses and auricula all fall into this category. You will notice the difference if you do perform these tasks, but again, if the performance is still good, leave well alone. The downside might be that the plants are smaller than they might be if grown in a border where there is no restriction on the root system. In other words you are naturally dwarfing them.

As a rule of thumb, unless stated otherwise on the plant labels, nearly all herbaceous plants are tolerant of lime, so use a soil-based compost John Innes No 2 for long-term planting schemes.

PRIMROSES

Members of the primrose family make excellent container plants, the most common being coloured primulas and multi-headed polyanthus planted along with spring bulbs. They grow in spring sunshine or light shade, but will prefer to be in full or light shade by mid summer. This is the clever part of container gardening, as the plants can easily be moved to the conditions which suit them best. They are often purchased as bedding plants in the autumn or spring and sadly are discarded once the first flowering season is over, which is a shame as they will live on for

OPPOSITE: *Dicentra spectablis alba* makes a good centrepiece for the table, while *Aquilegia* 'William Guinness' is planted in the pot to the right.

several years. They remain evergreen in moist conditions.

The primrose family is easy to use in individual pots, to be enjoyed on their own, or with other plants in larger pots, troughs and hanging baskets. This is certainly true for the common wild primrose *Primula vulgaris*, which looks so pretty flowering in the spring either on its own or along with sweet violets *Viola odorata*. Together they are harbingers of spring. The addition of *Fritillaria meleagris*, the dainty bulb known as the snake's head fritillary, adds a little extra height but takes none of the frailty away. The result is charming and very natural.

Various primrose cultivars have emerged over the years including *Primula* 'Francisca', which was discovered on a traffic island in Canada. It is unusual because it has green flowers with a pale yellow eye. It blooms for several weeks from mid to late spring and into early summer, and as a cut flower will stay fresh for ten to twenty days

The gold-laced primroses are rather more old-fashioned, and certainly appealing with their gold eyes, black petals and gold edges. Sometimes they are sold with maroon or purple petals but with the same lacing effect.

From the mountains of Europe, *Primula auricula* is a further species within the primrose family. Auriculas are very popular at the garden shows but have a reputation for being difficult to manage. Exquisite to look at, either with 'self-coloured' petals of maroon, deep red, yellow, blue or purple, some auriculas are known as 'fancy' with frills or edges of grey, green or red. Some are doubles; these will be later to flower. Some have a

ABOVE: ***Primula* 'Francisca'** has ruffled green flowers and a central yellow eye, making it very unusual among the primrose family.

BELOW: **This is a charming combination using the wild primrose *Primula vulgaris* with sweetly scented purple and white violets *Viola odorata*; the snake's head fritillary bulb *Fritillaria meleagris* is a welcome optional addition providing extra height and beauty.**

Primula 'Gold-Laced Group' is a stunning polyanthus type of primrose with several flowers to every stem; each bloom has a gold eye, black petals and gold edges. It is almost too good to mix with anything else.

Primula auricula makes a beautiful single specimen plant for a small pot. It can also be planted in conjunction with small spring bulbs such as these broad-leaved *Muscari latifolium*.

beautiful grey dusting of farina on the leaves or petals giving a frosted look. Several have a honey scent. They will live for many years, so long as they have good drainage, achieved by adding extra grit to the compost. Take care not to over-water in the summer and keep them on the dry side during the winter when the plants become more or less dormant. It is also best to shade them against high summer sunshine. They are super in small to medium sized pots, either on their own or mixed with small bulbs such as *Fritillaria meleagris* and grape hyacinths.

Another relation is *Primula veris*, the common cowslip which in the wild prefers the open mead-ows. With its dangling bells, it makes a very pretty choice for a hanging basket, flowering for several weeks in late spring, and associates rather well with hostas which will just be emerging as the cowslip is flowering. Then as the summer days lengthen it will be the hosta which will be centre stage, until next spring when the roles will reverse. It also looks good surrounded by *Gallium odoratum* commonly known as sweet woodruff, a low carpeting plant which produces dainty sprays of white flowers in late spring and keeps its leaves all winter. This combination looks good in either a hanging basket or pot, and they will thrive side by side for many years.

All these members of the primrose family will profit from dividing in the autumn using fresh compost. They will soon recover and flower generously the following spring. Beware vine weevils – the grubs will devour the roots – so it is advisable to use an anti-vine weevil treatment of either Provado or nematodes in spring and again in late summer.

AQUILEGIAS

Aquilegias, commonly known as columbines or granny's bonnets, are short-lived deciduous perennials, but despite this they make very good container plants with their pretty blue, white, or sometimes yellow flowers in early summer, good seedheads and handsome grey-green foliage throughout the summer and into autumn.

They grow in full sun or partial shade, but height may vary between 15cm for the dwarf varieties to over 75cm with the taller types. The dwarf kinds are excellent in alpine troughs while the taller ones are better in medium-sized pots. The taller *Aquilegia vulgaris* is a cottage garden favourite from which several well-known cultivars are derived. One of the most striking of these is 'William Guinness' sometimes sold as 'Magpie', a mix of deep velvety purple and white. Aquilegias make a handsome plant grown on their own; but in common with heucheras, the taller ones provide attractive low foliage for summer flowering lilies.

DICENTRAS

Bleeding heart or Dutchman's breeches are two of the intriguing common names of *Dicentra spectabilis* which is a native of eastern Asia. A

Left: *Dicentra spectablis* 'Alba' is a wonderful candidate for a container, especially if it can be raised up so that the shape of the overall plant as well as the individual flowers can be fully appreciated; it is planted here with sweet woodruff *Gallium odoratum*. The arching sprays look attractive backlit (*below left*), but also show up well against a dark background (*below right*).

cottage garden favourite, this is a deciduous perennial growing to a height of about 60cm with a 60cm spread in a pot. The exquisitely shaped pink flowers dangle from arching stems and create a wonderful spectacle in early summer, especially if the pot is raised up on a table or bench. Seen at eye level, then the entire shape of the plant can be fully enjoyed.

It grows well in partial shade but will also thrive in a sunnier spot so long as the compost is kept moist. Try to find a sheltered position as the stems can spoil in strong winds. It intensely dislikes root disturbance, so if you think you would ever like to move it on to a slightly bigger container choose the shape of your pot carefully; use one with straight or flared sides but definitely with no shoulders, else removal from the pot will be difficult. Once planted it should be happy for years, if slugs and snails and vine weevil are kept at bay. It has a long dormancy from late summer to early spring so you may prefer to underplant with an evergreen perennial such as sweet woodruff *Gallium odoratum* to give winter interest and also to provide a carpet of white flowers whilst the dicentra, be it pink or white *D. s.* 'Alba', is flowering above.

SOLOMON'S SEAL

Solomon's seal *Polygonatum × hybridum* is a deciduous perennial thriving in a shady or partially shady site. Its graceful arching stem bears exquisite white bells, flushed with green, which dangle down in clusters in late spring and early summer. It will reach up to 1m high in a container. Although it is said to prefer a fertile, humous-rich, moist soil, it is also one of those plants which after it has flowered will take nine months of quiet neglect. By this comment, please don't ignore it, but you won't have to be feeding and watering constantly; just make sure the compost is kept moist to the touch during the summer and autumn months. It will happily grow and perform for years in the same pot, maybe ten or fifteen years, although eventually you will want to divide it for fear of it spreading so wide and breaking the pot. The dormant

Solomon's seal *Polygonatum × hybridum* will stay in the same pot for very many years, gradually building up a strong colony of maybe forty or more arching stems, which are excellent material for flower arrangers.

late winter/early spring months are the time to divide it.

Its main problem is that it might be attacked by the grey Solomon's seal sawfly caterpillar (*Phymatocera aterrima*) in early summer; generally this happens soon after flowering. Prompt picking off of the caterpillars will arrest the problem, and if you happen to miss them, all is not lost, as next year the plant will perform again quite happily. Otherwise, spray with a specific systemic insecticide.

Why bother planting it in a container? Well, this is one of those plants which are so much better appreciated in a pot rather than in a border where its pretty flowers are so often hidden by its leaves. Raised up in a pot, it is like a living flower arrangement. It is then that you can really appreciate those arching sprays. For the adventurous, cultivars to seek out are 'Striatum' with variegated leaves, and 'Betberg' with bronze purple leaves when young. But it is actually hard to beat the common plain green form.

VARIEGATED GROUND ELDER

Variegated ground elder *Aegopodium podagraria* 'Variegatum' might sound a nightmare to those who have tried to eradicate the normal all-green version from their borders. But the creamy markings on the variegated form make this an easy and attractive plant for a container in partial shade.

Its only vice is that it sulks if the compost dries out in the summer months, but it will quickly revive after being watered. It will cheerfully stay in the same container for years, reliably sending up fresh young shoots each spring. Flowering is spasmodic, and just to make sure it does not self-seed around in nearby borders, remove the seed-heads before they have matured.

HOSTAS

Hostas are popular deciduous herbaceous perennials, often used as a container plant thriving mostly in shade or partial shade, although a few will grow in full sun depending on the cultivar selected. As a plant group, it offers a wide range of leaf shape, size of leaf, variegation and colour varying from gold to blue. The flowers are usually strong to pale lilac or white, sometimes scented.

Their main drawback is that slugs, and even worse snails, think that hostas are a fantastic fodder plant, and so the beautiful leaves soon turn into ragged shadows as early summer unfolds. Hence their use in containers, raised up and partially out of reach particularly if a barrier

Variegated ground elder *Aegopodium podagraria* 'Variegatum' provides a welcome lift to a dark corner of the patio or balcony; trapped, tough and reliable, it can remain in the same container for very many years.

In just a couple of years this *Hosta* 'Golden Tiara' has completely filled the space and makes a sumptuous spring and summer show in this 36cm diameter lined wicker hanging basket.

of copper banding, broken seashells or even egg shells is set up. Adding a lot of extra sand, say 20 per cent, to the potting mix will help guard against the dreaded vine weevil whose larvae do so much damage to hosta roots, but still beware.

Hostas can be grown as a sole planting scheme, with the size of the container chosen to suit the size of the leaf which can vary from mini (up to only 15cm as in 'Mini Blue'), through small, medium, large to giant dinner plate size as in chalky blue 'Big Daddy', as well as the commensurate spread. Just one pot on its own can look super; a pair either side an entrance gate can look stunning; while a whole collection of different shapes and leaf colours will create a fantastic array under the eaves of a house, on a shady balcony, or in the shade of a wall. Just watch out for slugs and snails; you might think you have created the perfect barrier but as the leaves grow, the plants might touch a wall and then access is made easy with a ladder system created over every plant.

So why not grow hostas in hanging baskets? Hosta leaves make a beautiful silhouette against a wall, and as the summer progresses their flowers arise to make a magnificent central display.

What's more, a suspended basket makes it a difficult place for all the dreaded pests to reach. Although it is a major trial for the slugs and snails, however, if the foliage touches the wall at any time the barrier is broken.

A good choice for small to medium hanging baskets are those of a small to medium stature such as *Hosta* 'Gold Edger' or 'Gold Rush' growing around 15–25cm tall. For a medium to large baskets try *Hosta* 'Golden Tiara' which grows around 40cm across, with creamy variegated leaves and lavender flower spikes; *Hosta* 'Fire and Ice' is also a good option, this time with striking white and green leaves and again with lavender flowers.

Hostas can be grown in pots and baskets along with other perennials with which they will compete for space quite happily. Depending on container size you might use two small hostas on either side of centre to form one bigger display or just one central medium-sized hosta.

They can be fronted with creeping jenny in its normal green form, or better still the golden form *Lysimachia nummularia* 'Aurea', which will quickly cascade over the sides, and has small

The young fronds of the lady fern make a wonderful shape with hostas, along with creeping jenny *Lysimachia nummularia* 'Aurea' and mimulus, which make good edgers and trailers.

Another plant which associates well with hostas is the monkey flower *Mimulus*. Planted around the edge of the container, it nicely softens the rim. Available in several shades of cream, pale pink, yellow and orange it makes an easy colour association with all hostas. Pink mimulus looks particularly striking with medium-sized *Hosta* 'Red October' which has russet red petioles or stems and green leaves with a bluish tint. This makes a good combination for a small to medium hanging basket or pot. Although the mimulus might not survive the winter, it should self-seed in situ and flower each year.

With medium-sized hostas chosen for either side of a large basket, then consider a fern for the middle back position. Pick the fern to suit the scale. In a large hanging basket where the diameter is 46cm, then the lady fern *Athyrium filix-femina* makes a great choice. You will find it grows rather smaller here in its limited space than it would in a garden border and will make a lovely companion planting scheme. It provides an exciting late spring picture as its new fronds unfurl, then a lovely expansive summer, autumn and winter sight as the fronds grow and flourish. The hosta leaves will have died by late autumn, but they will re-emerge next spring. Only strong winds or drying soil will spoil the fern display. The fern fronds are best cut back in late winter so that you can enjoy the spring spectacle unhindered by old foliage.

HEUCHERAS

Heuchera is another popular plant for pots. Evergreen and capable of enjoying sun or partial shade, it has pretty delicate flower spikes, and heuchera plants are now available in an ever-expanding range of leaf colours and markings from lime green, russet, through to purple, grey and black. Generally the lighter colour leaves prefer more shade, as they can get scorched if the sun is too strong. The height is generally around 30cm with a spread of around 40cm so this makes an ideal size for most medium pots. Try to position the dark and silver leaved varieties where they can be seen with the low evening sun behind

yellow cup-shaped flowers in summer. Deemed an evergreen perennial, in hanging baskets its trails are less robust and are usually best cut off when they begin to look ragged after mid winter winds have played their part. They will soon shoot again in the spring. It thrives in moist conditions in sun or partial shade, though the golden form can scorch if the sun is too hot and the compost too dry.

Another good edger is a summer flowering viola such as pale blue 'Maggie Mott' or black 'Mollie Sanderson'. You can also add a gold-splashed form of London pride *Saxifraga* x *urbium* 'Aureopunctata' which will provide an attractive evergreen carpet and flowers in May, just as the hosta leaves emerge.

RIGHT: *Heuchera* 'Midnight Rose' makes an excellent all year round container display, and looks especially attractive as seen here in glazed blue pots.

RIGHT: *Heuchera* 'Midnight Rose' makes an excellent all year round container display, and looks especially attractive as seen here in glazed blue pots.

BELOW: *Heuchera* 'Silver Scrolls' has two-toned leaves, silver on one side, plum on the reverse.

them; the leaves will glow like embers. The underside of the leaves is very attractive and, seen reversed, they are worthy of use in a table flower arrangement.

After two or three years, heucheras will appear to grow upwards out of the soil. Simply repot deeper to reinvigorate the plant or, in the autumn or early spring, remove some of the side shoots with fine root hairs attached and replant to create new plants. They are not troubled by slugs or snails; however, vine weevil can be a problem.

Heucheras are most worthy as a single specimen plant or as a mixed planting. Several have wonderful purple foliage, including the old favourite 'Plum Pudding' with its mottled plum purple leaves; 'Midnight Rose' is deep maroon with pink flecks; 'Liquorice' is almost black. The flower spikes are tall and wispy and make very dainty displays with tiny white or pink blooms in early summer. All heucheras, but especially the dark leaved forms, look super in association with late flowering tulips or with summer flowering lilies such as *Lilium* 'Pink Perfection' or 'Regale'.

ERIGERON

For sun-loving, summer-flowering plants which are long in flower and easy to look after in containers, then the erigeron family is hard to beat. Best of all is the tiny Mexican daisy *Erigeron karvinskianus* with its dainty white flowers which fade to rose; it thus creates a two-toned effect throughout the summer and autumn. It is a wonderful choice to add around the edge of pots where the main subject may be more structural, as with many of the succulents including agaves. On the other hand it also suits more see-through plants such as grasses; it looks particularly charming planted below Japanese blood grass *Imperata cylindrica rubra*. It will often self-seed in gravel or amongst paving which can be a real blessing, creating a pretty frill around the pot. It will overwinter quite happily outdoors, or where planted with tender succulents it will be happy in the protection of a greenhouse for the winter. All it

An airy selection of *Erigeron* 'Dimity', silver-leaved *Festuca glauca* and trailing *Sedum reflexum* make a pretty summer display in this metal Afghan rice pot which has been adapted by having holes drilled in the base. It is raised on thin metal supports bringing the flowers closer to eye level adding to the frailty of the planting scheme.

needs is a simple haircut in late winter, merely trimming it back to within a few centimetres of the root structure.

Erigeron 'Dimity' is a little more substantial in appearance and will grow to around 30cm, with bigger flowers which start as pinky-mauve with orange eyes and buds, making an unusual combination. Flowering in June and July, they make an attractive partner for small steely blue grasses such as *Festuca glauca*. They do not appear to be self-seeders like their Mexican cousins. Trim the flowers back as they begin to fade to ensure a succession of colour. They have an evergreen rosette of leaves and are best divided in early spring, although they will survive quite happily for several years without any fuss.

ECHINACEA

Echinacea have become popular plants in recent years. They are sun loving, but will also perform well in partial shade, easy to maintain, long flowering from mid to late summer and into the autumn, with many new colours now available including yellows, green and orange. They are an excellent way to attract butterflies onto your patio.

One to look out for is 'Fatal Attraction' with its deep pink flowers and dark, almost black, stems; another is 'Green Envy', a subtle fusion of green and purplish pink flowers. These will both grow up to 75cm tall or more, so are best planted in large containers. However, there are others which are more compact and make excellent subjects for medium pots such as double 'Coconut Lime' with its pom-pom of pale creamy green florets surrounded by a ring of white petals. Its stems are sturdy and remain upright. It makes a super container specimen rarely reaching much more than 50cm.

HELLEBORES

Hellebores are a major contributor to the winter patio, coping with low light conditions and shade, producing some exquisite flowers.

Helleborus niger, known as the Christmas rose, flowers from mid to end winter, but it grows only 30cm high and is often spoilt by slugs or soil splash in the garden. Raised up in a pot or even a hanging basket and seen at eye level, it really becomes a star attraction. Plant it with some variegated trailing ivy to soften the edge of the container.

Echinaceas are a good source of nectar for butterflies, as seen here with this tortoiseshell on *Echinacea* 'White Swan'.

The double *Echinacea* 'Coconut Lime' is more compact than most echinaceas and makes an interesting choice for mid to late summer interest in a pot.

Male fern *Dryopteris filix-mas* is planted in an old butler's sink which was treated with peat, sand and cement to give it a 'stone' effect. It was placed here to hide a manhole cover and has not been replanted for twenty years.

The same transformation can occur with *Helleborus orientalis* which hides its beauty under its dangling heads. Raise it up by growing it in a pot, and then raise the pot onto a table or windowsill and you have a much easier way to enjoy its charms. Also known as the Lenten rose, it will flower from early spring. To show off the flowers remove any tattered leaves as the flowers first emerge in late winter.

Helleborus foetidus is also useful, blooming with felty grey-green flowers from mid winter until spring. It grows taller than the others, so grow it in a large pot with a mixture of early and late flowering daffodils. It will thrive in sun or shade. It is shorter lived than the other two forementioned and may need replacing every autumn, but with luck by then you might have seedlings growing nearby.

FERNS

Ferns are amongst the most ornamental of all foliage plants, requiring little extra care beyond two guidelines. First is to keep the plants in shade or partial shade, and second to maintain moist conditions. Some are evergreen and need only a late winter clean-up, with the removal of the leaf fronds down to the base of the plant in order to reveal the exquisite new fronds which will emerge in spring. A few are deciduous and die down in late autumn.

Although ferns will not produce attractive flowers like so many of our common garden plants, they are very worthy of containers as specimen plants in their own right or mixed with others. Architectural, easy to look after with no trouble from slugs, snails or vine weevils, long lived in pots and baskets, extremely attractive, perfect for difficult shady places – ferns have to be one of the top plants for pots, troughs, and hanging baskets. They are perfect for those who prefer a quiet, calming all-green look, associating well with ivies and hostas. They will happily remain in their containers for very many years, so use John Innes No 2, a soil-based compost.

For a large trough or barrel, consider the male fern *Dryopteris filix-mas*. It can reach up to 1.5m in the right conditions, but in a container is much more likely to be under 1m in height or spread. It makes a useful evergreen screen for

The female fern *Athyrium filix-femina* creates an elegant partnership in a large hanging basket with golden Creeping Jenny *Lysimachia nummularia* 'Aurea' cascading over the sides – ideal for a shady spot under the canopy of a tree, in this case a lilac.

Athyrium 'Ghost', a deciduous fern with elegant silver-green fronds each with a red midrib, makes an excellent choice for this green glazed pot under the shade of a birch tree.

covering an ugly manhole cover. Plant on its own, or if the container is large enough consider a tall foxglove and maybe a large hosta as its companions. Like many other ferns on its own it will tolerate drier conditions, but if you create a mixed planting scheme you will have to be aware of the other plant requirements.

For a medium-sized pot then try the Cornish fern *Polypodium x Mantoniae cornubiense* (syn. *Polypodium vulgare cornubiense*) which is evergreen and grows up to around 45cm in height with a similar spread. It often produces a mixture of slightly different shaped fronds, which creates an interesting look. Late to come into new leaf, it won't look shabby in the spring. Indeed this is one of the best looking ferns for the autumn right through the winter and well into spring.

The female fern *Athyrium filix-femina* is one of the best for containers. It is evergreen and reaches 30–75cm tall in a pot or large hanging basket. It can be used on its own to make a wonderful all year round display, or associates well with medium hostas and creeping jenny.

The Japanese painted fern *Athyrium nippon icum pictum* has attractive colourings ranging from wine red to silver on its leaves, which grow to around 45 with a spread of 60cm or more. It prefers a moist sheltered position and looks graceful in a hanging basket as well as a pot. It is deciduous so will not provide any winter interest. Another deciduous fern definitely worth trying is *Athyrium* 'Ghost' which is a cross between the colourful Japanese fern and the elegant lady fern. Its fronds are pale silvery green, with red midribs which heighten the effect. In extreme winters, it is probably best to either protect the crowns of these two ferns or bring them under a potting shed where they can be kept on the dry side.

5 BULBS

Bulbs play a magnificent part in container gardening. They add such flair and flamboyance even in the depths of winter, whilst in spring, summer and autumn they are at their most brilliant.

Bulbs are a means of storing food reserves in long periods of drought and thus are perfect for pots and baskets on the patio where they can excel in their main season and then drift into a quite dormancy. The term 'bulb' here refers to the following: true bulbs such as snowdrops, daffodils, tulips, lilies and nerines; *corms* such as crocus and gladioli; *rhizomes* such as cannas; and *tubers* such as eranthis, cyclamen and begonias. Agapanthus are also included; though not strictly a bulb, they do have very fleshy roots which act as a water storage device. Just as with any other plant group, some are fully hardy so that they can be left outside all year round, while some of the summer flowering ones are tender, with the need for frost-free conditions in the winter.

There are two main seasons of planting bulbs for containers. First, autumn is the time to plant the winter and spring flowering displays including snowdrops, hyacinths, daffodils and tulips, plus any instant autumn bulbs such as *Cyclamen* 'Miracle'. Second, spring is the time to plant the summer-flowering displays such as lilies, begonias, agapanthus, cannas and nerines. Some of these are hardy and can be planted outdoors right from the start. Others are tender and should be started in the protection of a greenhouse or conservatory. For all the winter work, or for summer bulbs which are left in situ outside all year round, use a soil-based John Innes No 2 compost which will provide a gritty medium and ensure good drainage, essential during winter frosts.

AUTUMN FLOWERING DISPLAYS

There are two fully hardy cyclamen that can be used for small autumn and winter pots outdoors. First *Cyclamen hederifolium* which will flower in the autumn but hold its beautiful veined leaves

OPPOSITE: *Tulipa* 'Pink Impression' planted with white foxglove, which will flower later.

RIGHT: *Cyclamen* 'Miracle', a miniature cyclamen, makes a great autumn display, often lasting with a little help in severe weather, right through to spring; then it can be saved for another season.

through to spring, and secondly *Cyclamen coum* which will produce exquisite leaves in the autumn but flower from mid to late winter. Both can be purchased as dry tubers in the autumn or as pots of growing plants and used as an instant display. Mix them with variegated ivies. Keep them in a shady spot for the summer.

A new cyclamen has become available for outdoor pots and window boxes in recent years, bred from *Cyclamen persicum* which is sold as an indoor winter houseplant. The new form is a miniature variety called *Cyclamen* 'Miracle', available in purple, red, white and pink, with the bonus of attractive leaves and a sweet scent – those with white flowers are the most fragrant. This is a versatile and welcome addition to the container world. Plant one to a small pot and grow on its own or with ivy. Or display a few pots together. Alternatively buy several and mass under a standard holly or bay. Primarily it should be regarded as an outdoor autumn container plant. In sheltered locations with only a few degrees of frost you might find that these will survive the winter and still be in flower in spring; but regard this is a bonus, not a guarantee. Fleece will help in severe weather, or simply bring them into a cool area of the house overnight, or leave outside in a porch or veranda. Offer them a dormant summer in the shade and they will come back into flower in the autumn.

WINTER

The main winter-flowering bulb display comes from snowdrops, winter-flowering aconites and very early daffodils, with support from crocus and iris. All these can bring colour to the patio. They can be planted on their own or in association with hellebores, ivy, winter-flowering heathers, colourful cornus and violas.

Winter-flowering aconites *Eranthis hyemalis*, one of the first bulbs to flower in the new year, and a good source of food for honeybees.

Winter-flowering aconites *Eranthis hyemalis* and snowdrops *Galanthus nivalis* make a cheery mid winter scene, with pussy willow twigs inserted into the snowdrop pots for added interest; the variegated grass *Carex* 'Evergold' complements the arrangement.

Snowdrops *Galanthus nivalis* and winter-flowering aconites *Eranthis hyemalis* are both attractive to bees, providing early nectar. Unfortunately, neither of them reliably flower from every bulb purchased in the autumn. The reason is that they do not like the lifting and drying out process necessary for garden centre storage, which is why they are often sold after flowering in spring as growing bulbs 'in the green' with leaves. Be that as it may, purchased and planted in autumn and mixed with other companions in a basket this may not matter; it will be lovely to see just a few cheery faces in the depths of winter.

An alternative plan is available, however, to those who have access to the same bulbs growing in their own garden. Snowdrops and winter-flowering aconites both move easily in early winter, so if you know where they are growing, carefully dig down to find them, and immediately transfer to small pots and baskets to grow on unhindered. They will look delightful by the back door, on a window sill, or in the porch where you can enjoy them at close quarters without the need to go down the frosty garden path. Simply plant them back in another part of the garden later in spring and start a new colony.

For very early daffodils, look out for creamy *Narcissus* 'Spring Dawn' and golden *N.* 'Rijnveld's Early Sensation' which both flower in mid to late winter. The bulbs themselves are quite large so you need a deep pot, which is useful as this will be the right scale for their growing height at around 30–35cm. Plant them with *Helleborus foetidus* which is also early to bloom and has soft grey-green flowers. Or try a 'half and half' planting scheme, this time using a large pot or half barrel. Plant a group of these early flowering daffodils at the front half of the pot, the hellebore in the middle and then add a group of later flowering daffodils such as *Narcissus* 'Pipit' at the back. When the first show is over, just turn the pot around and enjoy the second show without the untidiness of the first daffodil's leaves, now flagging and hidden behind the hellebore which will still be in flower.

Crocus tommasinianus is known as the snow crocus and has lilac mauve blooms which look delightful in the late winter sunshine. Left in the same container for a number of years it will slowly increase to produce a carpet of colour only 10cm high.

On the other hand dwarf *Iris reticulata* are probably best considered as short-term flowering

Flowering in early spring, multi-headed *Narcissus* 'Tete-a-Tete' is long lasting and reliable, useful for small pots as the display is generous from just a few bulbs; 'Howera' would make a good option for mid spring.

This is a charming pot of wild flowers with snake's head fritillary *Fritillaria meleagris*, primroses and scented violets.

Hyacinthus 'Jan Bos' provides flair and scent and makes a good companion with *Chionodoxa forbesii* and *Saxifraga* × *urbium* 'Aureopunctata' in a long-term hanging basket.

in late winter, with blue or purple on their petals; royal blue 'Harmony' and dark purple 'Pauline' are two distinctive choices. Meanwhile *Iris danfordiae* has yellow petals which show up well. All these iris will only grow to around 15cm.

SPRING

In early spring dwarf daffodils are truly delightful in small to medium size containers on the patio, or porch or window sill. They can be mixed endlessly with different colour violas and prim-roses as well as small bulbs such as crocus, scillas, anemone blanda, hyacinths and grape hyacinths. *Narcissus* 'February Gold' is a great one to use, with its long trumpet and reflexed petals. It is short, sturdy and long lasting in flower. Underplant with large Dutch crocus such as white 'Jean d'Arc' or purple 'Remembrance'. *N.* 'Jetfire' has golden flyaway petals and an orange trumpet and makes an excellent choice for a container, terracotta or glazed. Multi-headed yellow *N.* 'Tete-a-Tete' is also popular – neat, long flowering and available to buy both as potted growing bulbs as well as dry bulbs in the autumn; plant it with wild or coloured primroses and ivies in a window box, wall pot or basket.

Other dwarf daffodils will flower slightly later, also coinciding with grape hyacinths, and hyacinths, the double early tulips and fritillarias. Glistening white *N.* 'Thalia' looks charming with Fritillaria meleagris, known as the snake's head fritillary or the guinea hen flower on account of its chequered markings. Or try the fritillarias as a naturalistic look with wild primrose *Primula vulgaris* and little scented violets *Viola odorata*. They each love a damp spring in sun or partial shade and are perfect together. The hyacinths are also in flower at this time, in all shades of blue, pink, white and salmon. There are some striking colours available including 'Jan Bos' which is a rich carmine red, and 'Woodstock' which is a deep burgundy. All are sweetly scented. They coincide with pretty blue *Chionodoxa forbesii* known as the glory of the snow, and the blue grape hyacinth *Muscari armenicaum*. All these bulbs will perform well in containers and, left undisturbed, should flower again next year.

By now some of the smaller Kaufmanniana tulips are in bloom including pink and white 'Heart's Delight' and salmon 'Shakespeare'. They combine well with the dwarf daffodils and grape hyacinths, violas, pink or red daisies and golden feverfew. This is also the time for the double early tulips such as delicate 'Viriflor' and pale pink 'Peach Blossom'. Sad to say, the double early tulips do not seem to repeat their glory reliably well the following year, so just enjoy

This small lined wicker basket is 25cm long × 20cm wide × 10cm deep and has been planted with eight *Tulipa* 'Peach Blossom', ten *Muscari armeniacum*, four *Viola*, one pink and one red double daisies *Bellis perennis*, and two variegated ivies to spill over the sides. It can be planted up in autumn; alternatively all these plants are available to buy from the garden centres in the early spring.

Muscari latifolium has become very popular with its rich two-toned flowers and tidy broad leaves; it associates well with mid spring dwarf daffodils and tulips.

Narcissus 'Bellsong' is a dainty choice for a hanging basket or wall pot in mid spring, with its salmon pink cup and its petals which fade from cream to white with age; ideal with *Muscari latifolium*.

them whilst in flower and buy more new bulbs in the autumn.

The grape hyacinth *Muscari armeniacum* is a beautiful addition to many spring pots; they look good on their own or mixed. Its only drawback is that if it is too richly fed, or in too much shade, its leaves get rather shaggy. The pale blue form called *M.* 'Valerie Finnis' is exquisite with *N.* 'Segovia', a delightful little daffodil with glistening white petals and a creamy miniature cup. Or try the broader leaf variety called *M. latifolium* with *N.* 'Bellsong', a dainty dwarf daffodil with a soft salmon pink centre. Either of these two combinations would grace a mid spring window box, hanging basket, or wall pot and survive intact for another year. Simply add new violas or bellis daisies next autumn, or if you used them the first season you might even find they have self-seeded.

Some of the later flowering tulips are very neat and delicate, with beautiful colourings. *Tulipa batalinii* 'Honky Tonk' is only 25cm high and has a rose flush on the reverse of its creamy yellow petals. It looks excellent with the later flowering dwarf daffodils such as 'Segovia', 'Bellsong', and 'Hawera'. *Tulipa clusiana* 'Lady Jane' is of similar size with a stronger pink stripe to its outer petals while inside is pure white. *Tulipa bakeri* 'Lilac Wonder' is even smaller at 8cm, pink on the outside, gold within. They combine well with violas, primulas and golden feverfew. For longevity of planting scheme use *Saxifraga* × *urbium* 'Aureopunctata', which provides such dainty flowers in late spring after the main bulb display is over. The pink tones of *Tulipa clusiana* 'Lady Jane' associate well with purple- or pink-leaved *Heuchera* 'Midnight Rose'. Here again the heuchera will flower for weeks in the summer while the tulips are building up their reserves for next year's flowering. All these small tulips are close to the species from which they were bred and will survive in containers for several seasons.

The daffodil season lasts from mid winter to late spring, and one of the best is multi-headed *Narcissus* 'Pipit', massing well to produce a generous display of distinctive lemon yellow flowers

RIGHT: *Tulipa clusiana* 'Lady Jane' and evergreen Heuchera 'Midnight Rose' create a lovely spring combination; the tulip will form good seedheads and the heuchera will produce dainty flowers in early summer.

BELOW: The multi-headed *Tulipa Bakeri* 'Lilac Wonder' is only 10cm high and tends to fall gracefully around the edge of a pot so would be a good subject for a wall pot or hanging basket.

The white and lemon tones of *Narcissus* 'Pipit' make a good partner for summer flowering snowflake *Leucojum aestivum*.

with a white centre. It is perfect for a medium to large pot and with its clean colours associates beautifully with the summer-flowering snowflake *Leucojum aestivum.* Kept moist during the spring, they live side by side for several years.

Some daffodils such as *Narcissus* 'Katie Heath', 'Reggae' and 'Romance' have white petals and pink trumpets or cups. This makes a delightful combination and is lovely to associate with *Dicentra spectabilis* 'Alba' which might grow independently in a pot nearby. White bellis daisies, or white violas would look good with them too.

If you want to try a long-term planting scheme where the bulbs are left in the pots for three years (before emptying and dividing them), try planting the top with some variegated London pride *Saxifraga* × *urbium* 'Aureopunctata', which is such a useful little plant for carpeting long-term winter pots. Fully hardy, it spreads quickly, is easy to

Narcissus 'Romance' with variegated London pride *Saxifraga* × *urbium* 'Aureopunctata'.

propagate by pulling off a little plantlet, and being variegated it has extra foliage interest. Best of all, it produces delicate sprays of tiny white flowers soon after the main bulb displays, effectively giving another few weeks of life to the spring containers.

Apply a liquid feed to the bulbs at the time of flowering or very soon thereafter, and remember to keep the compost moist as they are now building up their food reserves for next year's show. The daffodil leaves will eventually die down, usually about six weeks after flowering is over. By then, the London pride will have finished flowering too. So this is the time to tidy up the dry daffodil leaves and remove the dead London pride flower stems. You will be left with a simple but attractive frill of variegated London pride until next spring.

The tall, late-flowering tulips with a height of 30–80cm are the jewels of spring containers. Their brilliant colours add flair to any patio. Choose pots which are deep enough to accommodate their larger bulb size, which means an inside depth of around 25cm, allowing for 5cm drainage and a 5cm gap between the top of the soil and the rim of the pot. The width will depend on the number of bulbs planted, but choose either medium or large in size. These taller tulips do not perform well a second year in containers, so treat them as a one-year stand only and start again next season. The general rule for these one-year displays is that you can plant bulbs as close together as you like so long as they are not touching. The full effect is fantastic. The bigger the pot, the greater will be the display. The use of several similar pots will also add to the drama.

There is the possibility of planting more than one kind of tulip in a pot so as to contrast the flower colours. Apeldoorn tulips can be red or yellow, and both could be planted in the same pot to flower together and produce a very arresting combination.

You also have the chance to lengthen the time of the display by staggering the time of flowering. *Tulipa* 'Negrita' with its purple beetroot flowers can be planted with double pink *Tulipa* 'Angelique', one of the truly great tulips. 'Negrita'

ABOVE: The London pride is now in flower while the leaves of the daffodil remain upright.

ABOVE: Here all three pots planted with *Tulipa* 'Negrita' are staged together: one has 'Negrita' alone; another includes 'Angelique'; and another includes black 'Queen of Night' as well as a dark purple wallflower. The pansies and wallflower will continue to flower until early summer.

BELOW: *Tulipa* 'Angelique' with its soft pink petals underplanted with pretty pale blue pansies; pale blue forget-me-nots would also work well.

BELOW: *Tulipa* 'Fontainebleau' is dressed for drama with its dark purple petals edged in white; white or pale blue forget-me-nots would make a good underplanting.

will flower first, overlap for a while with 'Angelique' which will then outlast it. Meanwhile black 'Queen of Night' can join the throng, or stately 'Fontainebleau', sumptuous 'Black Parrot', cup-shaped, deep maroon-black 'Paul Scherer' or double 'Black Hero'. These are all late flowering.

To give even more sparkle to the tulips, add some bedding plants, using pansies in over twenty self-colours and bi-colours, wallflowers from yellow, gold, red and pink; and forget-me-nots, either pale blue, white or pink. Any of them make ideal partners to show off the tulip colours. The combinations are as exciting as they are endless.

Another method of making the pot of tulips continue to provide interest into early summer is to plant a foxglove in the centre. The tulips will finish flowering, but then the foxglove will come into bloom for many weeks providing added height with elegant spires of white or pink or apricot flowers. When the show is over the pot can be emptied ready for a new display. The grey-green foliage of the foxglove works well with the softer pink tulips such as 'Pink Diamond', 'Mistress' and 'Apricot Beauty'. It also sits well with *Tulipa* 'Spring Green' which is a superb combination of pale green and creamy white, sometimes described as ivory. White pansies are just too bright for it, while foxglove foliage is perfect and allows the tulip to do all the talking.

SUMMER

The summer flowering bulbs are also super for containers where they can be shown off to their

Agapanthus like to be congested at their roots in order to flower well.

Agapanthus 'Venezuela' is evergreen with wide strappy leaves, long sturdy stems and extremely large heads which need staking. They are wonderful deep intense blue, and insects love to visit them for their nectar. Named because the seed came from Venezuela, this cultivar is probably derived from *Agapanthus africanus africanus*.

Lilium 'Golden Splendour'.

Lilium 'Pink Perfection'.

full glory. Containers are so clever in this respect. They raise the plants up to show them off, isolate them from borders, allow us to play with their colours both through the container and with their partners, and if they are tender or on the cusp of tenderness they allow us to give protection from the elements.

Agapanthus vary in hardiness. The evergreen varieties will prove the more tender. A frost-free winter is all the protection they require along with light, so a greenhouse is ideal. They all prefer a sunny spot. The deciduous type will prove more resilient to cold weather but still they would prefer some protection, such as a spot beside a warm house wall or a porch. They like their fleshy roots being congested which means that the roots should be bulging in the pots to get them to flower well. Eventually, after years of spectacular flowers, they will cease to bloom as well. This is the time to move them on into a larger pot. It will take a while to rebuild their strength, but soon they will be magnificent again. It makes life easier to use a straight-sided pot rather than one with shoulders, which impedes easy access to the roots. For this reason, you may find it easier to use a plastic pot to plant in, but for display purposes insert it into another fancier pot.

There are many cultivars to choose from: some with white flowers such as 'White Dwarf' which grows to only 50–60cm making it very manageable for a pot, and others with various shades of blue. 'Midnight Star' is a dark violet blue which

grows to around 80cm high, so it might need some discreet staking unless it is in a very sheltered spot away from wind. These two are both relatively hardy. In the autumn remove the dead leaves and stems of the deciduous varieties, and just tidy the flowering stalk and any old leaves from the evergreen types. Apply a liquid feed every fortnight from late spring until the flowers start to open.

Lilies are a great favourite to plant in pots on the patio where they will create a magnificent blaze of colour in mid summer and provide a rich scent. There are many to choose from, but for those who want a consistently good show year after year then try three trumpet-flowered ones: choose between stunning yellow 'Golden Splendour', dusky 'Pink Perfection' or white *Lilium* 'Regale'.

These lilies are all tall growers for partial shade or full sun, although they prefer shade at the base of the pot. Despite their 1m height, their flexible strong stems mean that they normally do not need staking. Plant as soon as available either in the autumn or in late winter; choose a deep pot three times the depth of the bulbs, using a gritty John Innes compost with extra grit spread immediately beneath each bulb to ensure good drainage. Allow 5cm between each bulb, and plant three to a pot. Dark purple or black heucheras look good with them all, providing evergreen foliage at the base and as the two flower together, the dainty heuchera flower spikes soften

Lilium 'Regale' with *Heuchera* 'Liquorice', whose wispy flowers soften the large lily trumpets.

the boldness of the lily trumpets picking up the darker shading on the back of the flowers. The bulbs can be left in their pots for two years or more, but remember to feed again the following year. You may find that *Lilium* 'Regale' self-seeds.

For those who are allergic to the lily pollen then help is at hand with the Asiatic double flowering varieties, sometimes called the kiss lilies, which have no scent and no pollen. They do very well in containers and are only about 60–70cm high so are easier to place than the taller ones. The bulbs are smaller and you may plant three or five to a pot. They flower earlier than the large trumpet varieties mentioned above. *Lilium* 'Fata Morgana' is the yellow form with upward facing flowers and maroon spots. The bulbs multiply well; divide and repot every three years.

Eucomis, commonly known as the pineapple lily on account of its shape, is another summer flowering bulb for sun or partial shade that will give spectacular results year after year. It is not reliably hardy in a container, although it can withstand some frost, so is best brought into a cool frost-free area for the winter months. There are various species available including *Eucomis bicolor* 'White Dwarf' with pale green flowers reaching about 40cm. *E. pallidiflora* is rather more dramatic and can reach 75cm.

Lilium 'Regale' is a stunning lily with beautiful maroon shadings on the outside of its scented trumpets, and attractive seedpods.

The best of all for stunning effect is *E. comosa* 'Sparkling Burgundy' with its beetroot coloured leaves which fade as the flowers begin to form. The flowers are a brilliant burgundy colour opening in succession over four to six weeks with a sweet scent. As fleshy seedpods form they still look attractive and eventually can be cut and used as dried flowers in the house. The seeds can be collected and sown. The leaves will die and the bulbs will go dormant for the winter. Allow them

Eucomis comosa 'Sparkling Burgundy' is a dramatic bulb for a mid to late summer display; its leaves are an intense dark burgundy when they first emerge, fading a little as flowering begins.

to be kept dry and start watering again as new foliage emerges in the spring. The bulbs of this cultivar will grow to a large size forming attached daughter bulbs around the original. One plant per pot is all that is required from the outset; plant 15cm deep and after two or three years move on into a larger pot so that the display can increase. A good partner if taken to a greenhouse for the winter is lampranthus with its starry bright pink, red or orange daisies. It will flower in late spring beside the emerging dark eucomis leaves.

Cannas are exotic subjects for large pots on the patio, with large spade-like leaves and tall spikes of orange, yellow or red flowers growing to around 1m tall. The leaves are normally green,

This sunny 41cm diameter hanging basket includes one upright pelargonium at the back, one upright non-stop begonia at the front, with two trailing begonias on either side and two trailing blue *Convolvulus sabatius*; this is the second year of the display.

but they can also be cream variegated as in 'Striata' or bronze striped as in 'Tropicanna'. A group of two or three pots together will add extra drama to your summer scene.

The canna rhizomes grow outwards in the pot, and every year or at least every second year will need dividing. Do this in late winter or early spring so that each new fleshy root has a tip with a growing eye. Use a John Innes No 2 compost, or a multi-purpose compost and add some long-term fertilizer. Don't be tempted to move the pots outside in late spring; wait until around midsummer's day if possible, to give them a better chance of flowering.

Water regularly during the growing period and feed fortnightly with a liquid fertilizer. Enjoy the foliage throughout the summer and the flowers from late summer until early autumn. Cut down the tall stems in the autumn to within 15cm of soil level and bring into a frost-free greenhouse for the winter. Recently, canna virus has become a problem, distorting the leaves, creating pale spots and debilitating the plant. There is no known cure. It is best to destroy any affected plants.

Begonias are another brilliantly colourful plant for summer containers. They are one of the most flexible of all to plant in a wide range of pot sizes as well as window boxes and hanging baskets. You can mix trailing begonias at the front with non-stop upright begonias behind for height. The colour choice is wide open with white, pink, red, yellow and orange all available. With some of the upright forms there is the additional choice of picotee edges to the flowers which make a super display. They will thrive in shade, partial sun or even a sunny spot, so they are one of the most useful of all container gardening plants, getting better and better as the summer merges into autumn.

Begonias can be purchased as dry tubers to be started off in mid spring in a greenhouse, or as growing plants in late spring. Plant the tubers convex side up, lightly pressing them into multi-purpose compost so that they rest on top.

They can be planted in a hanging basket for just one season either on their own or with other bedding plants, for example with lobelia, busy lizzies and nasturtiums around the edge. The nasturtiums will flower in early summer leaving the begonias to take over until the first frosts of autumn. Then all the plants can be discarded. But, if you have a frost-free greenhouse, and you choose perennial partners for your basket then they can all be overwintered. The planting partners could include trailing begonias, an upright pelargonium (geranium), and trailing blue *Convolvulus sabatius* all of which can be left in situ and enjoyed again the following year. So this year's hanging basket can be brought out next year as well. The begonia tubers will have grown bigger and the floral display will be even better. With attention to watering and regular liquid feeding, a third year of colour can also be enjoyed. The same can be true if you plant begonias with fuchsias. A real treat is to plant an orange trailing begonia or an 'Orange Picotee' at the base of *Fuchsia* 'Thalia' or 'Coralle' (*see* Chapter 2).

Smaller pots of individual plants can also look effective either all in one type of pot or for an informal look using a mixture of terracotta and glazed. They certainly look cheerful here on this colourful stepladder with rainbow slinky springs dangled down the sides. It is a shady north-facing spot but with the bright colours and mirror above, the display lifts the gloom and is very long lasting. Better still, all the begonias can be enjoyed next year.

6 ORNAMENTAL GRASSES

This chapter covers both ornamental grasses and sedges. Both are flowering plants that are wind pollinated. Grasses have hollow stems while sedges have a solid stem. Most of the ones mentioned here are perennial (both deciduous and evergreen), and nearly all are hardy, although, as ever, there are some exceptions.

Ornamental grasses and sedges are brilliant for containers and deservedly popular. There is a wide range to choose from, giving different shapes and leaf colour and, while never brightly coloured, some flowers can be exceptionally attractive. This is especially true if you can find a place where the sun is behind them so that the flowers and leaves are backlit.

They add hugely to any patio collection with so much to offer in the way of elegance, movement, character, and long-lasting effect. Try them

OPPOSITE: Three *Stipa tenuissima* make a simple but repeat planting scheme for these old wash dollies; they turn golden in the late summer and last right through to late winter.

BELOW: *Carex 'Evergold'* is simply one of the easiest and best choices of grasses for containers; even in the very depths of winter it will provide a cheery display along with snowdrops *Galanthus nivalis* and the Cornish fern *Polypodium* × *Mantoniae cornubiense*.

with a minimalistic style, grown on their own. They are easy to use as individual specimens, either as a single pot or as a small group. But for an exuberant, warm and intricate effect combine them with other plant groupings including shrubs, bulbs, perennials and succulents. Place them on a paved patio or enjoy them on gravel. They look attractive in all sorts of containers including terracotta, whether plain or glazed, rusty metal, aluminium or wood; some of the low hummocky grasses even make good hanging basket displays.

SEDGES

Many of these grasses and sedges are very versatile growing in sun and partial shade. Of them all, *Carex* 'Evergold' must rank near the top for consistency. It is an evergreen sedge with light gold and green foliage growing to 20–25cm; as

such it will provide twelve months of interest in pots and hanging baskets. Easy to look after, this is one of those 'real good doers'. Try a repeating pattern with a few pots together, making golden hummocks around the terrace. Add small pots of winter and spring bulbs amongst them; try ferns or hellebores. Then in summer, move pots of tender plants besides them, such as soft blue Swan River daisy *Brachyscome*, white bacopa *Sutera* or busy lizzies *Impatiens* to create a different scene.

The carex family is extensive. *Carex dolichostachya* 'Kaga-nishiki' is similar to 'Evergold' but has narrower lemon-striped leaves. It grows to 25cm and flowers in early summer. It associates well with the soft foliage of *Euphorbia cyparissias* 'Fen's Ruby', a low-growing perennial with flushed purple foliage and lime green flowers. Another very good one to choose is *Carex testacea*, which is a little taller growing to 40–50cm. Also evergreen, it has the advantage of orange-green foliage with subtle changes in colour through the summer, and by autumn the colouring is warm, rich and extremely attractive. Terracotta pots are ideal, but rich rusty metal containers are also good, especially for any grasses with orange tones in their leaves. It is frost hardy, so give protection or keep it fairly dry in winter. It prefers partial shade but can also cope with a sunny spot.

Ophiopogon planiscapus 'Nigrescens' is a hardy sedge, this time with black strappy leaves. It is slow growing to around 15–20cm, suitable for sun or partial shade. Its flowers are followed by shiny black berries which make an attractive autumn feature. Low growing and evergreen, it looks smart throughout the year and makes a good partnership with very small bulbs such as cyclamen, snowdrops, aconites, crocus, dwarf daffodils and tulips which may be grown in separate pots nearby.

Ophiopogon planiscapus 'Nigrescens' makes a dramatic mound of dark foliage which changes little during the seasons.

TOP: *Rhynchospora latifolia* is a good subject for growing around the shallow margins of a pond.

BELOW: Gleaming in the sunlight *Pennisetum setiferum* 'Rubrum' looks distinctive in a 30cm diameter glazed mirror pot.

Normally, evergreen grasses and sedges are merely combed out to get rid of dead leaves in the spring. With *Carex* 'Evergold' and *Ophiopogon*, however, this may not be necessary for two or three years. When they begin to look a bit shaggy, better then to give them a complete haircut in the early growing season – that is to say early summer so they have time to recover and make good new growth before the autumn.

Star sedge *Rhynchospora latifolia* has slender leaves and tall white flowers surrounded by white bracts. It has a long flowering season from mid-summer until autumn. It likes boggy conditions and will cope on the shallow margins of a pool so that the base of the pot is just under the water. Cover with a layer of grit or sea shells, in order to avoid soil being splashed into the pond water in a heavy rainstorm. It is evergreen and native of Florida, and it is best to give it winter protection by bringing it into a light frost-free place where it will continue flowering for a few more weeks, so keep it barely moist at this time. Remove old flower spikes after flowering is finished, and cut back greenery in spring which will then allow tidy new growth to emerge. Move back outside once all risk of frost has past. It will eventually grow to 30–45cm tall and spread to around 60cm.

GRASSES

Another plant which needs winter protection is *Pennisetum setiferum* 'Rubrum'. This is a magnificent fountain grass from West Africa producing deep bronze leaves and lovely arching stems of fluffy flowers. It will cope with sunny dry conditions, making it ideal for containers, whether rusty metal, plain terracotta or glazed. Depending on the length of its growing season, it might reach between 50cm and 100cm. The slightest breeze will make the flowers sway to and fro. It really is a delightful plant. Unfortunately it is half hardy so it is best overwintered in a dry, frost-free place, or else you can treat it as an annual and sow seeds in spring or buy new plants in early summer.

All members of the pennisetum family are deciduous and should be given winter protection.

They are useful for containers, including *Pennisetum* 'Hameln' and 'Cassian's Choice' which both create mounds of foliage 80–90cm or so high and wide, and produce fluffy foxtail-like flowers in early autumn. Then the leaves turn a wonderful russet and the whole effect is quite beautiful. Follow the general rule of deciduous grasses by cutting them back close to soil level before growth starts again in the spring.

Lagurus ovatus has downy white pom-pom flowers which give it the common name of bunny tails or hare's tail grass. It is found around the Mediterranean and has become naturalized in many southern parts of the coastal UK and Eire. But beware, this is an annual grass, so it has to replaced each year. It can reach up to 25–30cm high and wide during the summer. The flower spikes are very distinctive, being a creamy white,

Pennisetum 'Cassian's Choice' is a form of *Pennisetum alopecuroides* commonly known as fountain grass renowned for its stunning display of late season flowers. The seedheads remain intact throughout the late autumn.

Lagurus ovatus produces dainty flower spikes, turning from pale green to creamy white with very soft long awns, hence the common name of Bunny Tails or Hare's Tail, seen here backlit catching the low evening sunlight beneath *Stipa tenuissima*.

and very soft with long awns. They appear over a long period giving a good succession of interest. Seeds can be sown outside into seed trays in mid-to-late spring or under cover in March. Germination should take ten to fourteen days. It is a favourite amongst children who love to touch the flowers. Grow it in a sunny position where morning or evening sunlight will bring it even more to life.

Other grasses which look super in containers on account of their distinctive flowers are the quaking grass family. In late summer, *Briza maxima* produces pale green flowerheads shaped like a lantern which rustle and quiver in the slightest breeze. It requires a sunny spot. Be aware, however, that it is an annual. Sow direct in the containers in which you want it to flower in soil-based compost in spring. It will grow around 75cm high. Its relative *Briza media* is a short-lived evergreen perennial, smaller in stature, reaching only 30cm high. Its flowerheads are smaller but pretty nevertheless, especially as with all these

A simple display of *Festuca glauca* which look attractive in these small terracotta pots along with the rusty metal basket.

type of grasses you can get the sunlight behind them so that the structure can be fully appreciated. The spangle grass *Chasmanthium latifolium* is another great choice, known for its dainty diamond-shaped flowers held on nodding stems. They dry well and make an attractive feature for weeks after flowering, turning from green, to bronze to tawny in winter. It is a deciduous perennial, reaches around 60–80cm or more in a container and likes full fun or partial shade.

Sometimes foliage is the key to the plant rather than the flowers. There is a group of blue grasses where the colour intensifies according to the amount of sunlight. In this respect *Festuca glauca* has much to offer. It is evergreen, neat, flowers well with heads held high above the foliage. In full sun, the leaves change from bluish green to steely silvery blue as the summer lengthens, making it one of the most striking of all grasses for small to medium pots. Create a small collection and display them together, maybe raised up on a table or bench to catch the sun. They can equally well be added alongside other grasses or succulents, where they will be the supporter, not the main player. Or mix them with small perennials such as trailing sedums and erigerons in the same container. *Festuca* 'Elijah's Blue' is one of the best forms, growing to around 30–40cm. *Festuca* 'Siskiyou Blue' at 40–50cm has slightly longer leaves, which create a mound-like appearance and is good in taller pots. *Festuca californica* is rather higher at 80–100cm, but the foliage is more open and upright. They look good in terracotta pots but equally handsome in metal containers. Although evergreen, trim the foliage right back in late winter.

Another blue grass, but considerably bigger at 75–90cm in a pot, is *Leymus arenarius* known as the lime grass. It is at home on sunny sandy dunes and has a tendency to run riot in a garden, but trapped in a pot it makes a wonderful specimen with its strappy blue leaves. It seldom flowers but the general exuberance more than makes up for that. It will happily remain in the same pot for years. It is deciduous so best cut back to the top of the pot in late winter. Try a pot of summer flow-

Leymus arenarius is growing here in an upturned rhubarb forcing pot in the middle of a gravel scree. The roots of the grass have anchored into the ground below so the pot itself has become fixed and stable.

Imperata cylindrica rubra is green in high summer but, in the full sun of late summer and early autumn, it then begins to turn red and lights up like a fiery cauldron.

ering lilies such as *Lilium* 'Pink Perfection' beside it – the colours will be wonderful.

By contrast, *Imperata cylindrica rubra*, commonly known as the Japanese blood grass, has red foliage, which starts in late summer at the tips of the leaves and then over the next few weeks the colour appears to drain downwards. It will grow to around 40cm tall and 30cm wide. It likes to be kept moist and will grow happily in sun or dappled shade; however, the best colouring will occur when it is placed in a sunny position. The leaves are semi-translucent so when the sun shines through it, the effect is magical. Consider raising it on a metal support or on a table. It will look wonderful on its own, or try planting the pretty white and pink Mexican daisy *Erigeron karvinskianus* around the edge. It is only frost hardy so needs some protection during the winter; a light, dry frost free-place such as a greenhouse or potting shed will be fine. The Mexican daisy will

cope with this routine as well. The grass is deciduous so cut the leaves back level with the top of the pot in late winter. Root prune or divide and re-pot every three years in early summer.

Hakonechloa macra 'Aureola' syn. 'Alboaurea', another grass from Japan, is useful for a site in sun or partial shade where its yellow leaves with their green and white stripes will sing out and offer a cheery effect, brighter and bolder in sun, paler and more subtle in shade. They produce a generous mounding effect, 35cm high and across. It needs moisture, so make sure it does not dry out. Use it as a pot plant on the terrace or as a specimen hanging basket plant. It is fairly slow growing so choose a small to medium pot for the first year and then pot on to a larger size the following spring. Violas can be planted around the edge to give extra interest for the first year. Cut back dead leaves during the winter ready for the spring awakening.

Stipa tenuissima is another excellent choice for small, medium or large containers, depending on the whether you use the grass on its own or with other plants. It is a short-lived perennial growing to around 40–50cm high. It is hardy, evergreen, likes full sun and will tolerate quite dry conditions so is a very useful container subject. It wafts around gently in the wind and is very soft to the touch, making it one of the most popular of all grasses both in garden and container use.

It flowers in early summer which is far earlier in the season compared with most grasses, giving it a much longer period of interest. The flowers are soft and delicate, and the whole plant will turn from soft green to gold to pale yellow as the season advances, making it just as valuable in winter as summer. It may self-seed in the ground below if standing on gravel, which could create an attractive naturalistic scene. Cut back to within just a few centimetres of soil level in late winter and allow the new growth to emerge clean and fresh. This is a grass which looks good on its own as a single specimen, or in a repeating pattern; it is captivating to see the fluffy flowerheads billowing in the slightest breeze. Or place several together in a large pot with other wispy herbaceous plants.

Miscanthus is a large family of deciduous grasses from Eastern Asia which are tough, long lived, flower well, and create great impact on the patio, holding their flowers right through the winter. Try to position them with their back to the sun so that their heads are held up like torches to the pale winter sunlight.

Many of them are rather tall at over 1.5–2m in garden soil, which might make a useful screen if so desired on a patio. However, as with most containerized plants, these grasses will probably not reach their full potential height in pots. A large container and attention to watering and feeding will be the best way to encourage them. Two of medium height are 'Rotsilber' which has the advantage of striking reddish flowers in late summer followed by very good autumn-coloured foliage, and 'Flamingo' which is a similar height but its dark pink flower heads hang gracefully giving a more mound-like appearance.

Hakonechloa macra 'Aureola' with its graceful mounding foliage makes an ideal choice for pots; reddish tints will occur in the autumn where grown in a sunny position, but if grown in partial shade the yellow colouring will be much paler.

The pale zinc colouring of the old wash dolly looks good with grasses. Here in late summer *Stipa tenuissima* has turned golden; the *Scabiosa columbaria ochroleuca* has pale yellow pincushion flowers; and below, the variegated grey and cream succulent *Sedum sieboldii* 'Mediovariegatum' adds contrasting form but similar colour to the container and grass.

Millium effusum 'Aureum' makes a bright golden display for a shady spot and contrasts nicely with the silvery blue grey fern *Athyrium* 'Ghost'.

If you prefer a lower variety then 'Yakushima Dwarf' is a selection to try, of which 'Elfin' with its narrow leaves and pinky red flowers is a great choice; it will probably reach about 1m in a pot. Other members of the family such as 'Cabaret' and 'Cosmopolitan' have striking white and green variegated leaves. Cut the foliage back in late winter level with or just above the top of the pot. Divide every three years in early summer.

Millium effusum 'Aureum' is known as Bowles golden grass after E.A. Bowles, the plant hunter, writer and botanical artist, who introduced it to cultivation. It is a golden form of a woodland grass and is therefore one of the few which actually prefers growing in shade or partial shade. As such it is a very useful name to add to the list of grasses for containers. It will grow around 60cm high and 30cm wide. With its soft golden leaves, it makes a welcome addition to the spring garden, emerging with the mid to late spring bulbs and becoming fully grown by early to mid summer when its leaves are more lime than yellow. It flow-ers from June to July. Depending on the winter temperatures it may be deciduous or semi-ever-green. It is a short-lived perennial which is easily divided in late spring. You might find seedlings in the ground around the plant which can be removed and planted elsewhere.

BAMBOOS

Grown well, bamboos will make super container plants and are able to provide excellent instant structure either to screen a view or just to add architectural presence to a garden setting. Bamboos are forest grasses, and although they are often seen growing in containers, they are not the easiest of plants to look after unless you can offer them plenty of shelter, and can be sure to never let them dry out in summer or winter. They will grow tall with lots of leafy growth at the top, which will make them rather unstable. So always use a good solid container to plant them in, one that sits squarely on the ground, and find a flat part of the patio to site them. This sounds obvious, but once planted the containers will be heavy to move unless you have a trolley, so working out the logistics from the outset makes good common sense.

Use a soil-based compost with extra grit to add to the weight. Slow release fertilizer is essential whenever you re-pot, and remember to give a liquid feed in late spring and summer. After a few years you may need to divide the roots in order to retain them within the container; this is a tough job and may require a saw. The roots could break a pot eventually so it is better to use a plastic liner within the pot from the beginning – then you can see if there are any danger signs of escaping roots. The plastic liner will also help to retain the moisture; otherwise use a plastic inner skin made out of recycled soil sacks. A wooden half barrel may offer one of the largest containers for you to use.

Those from the fargesia family, with their smaller tougher leaves, will thrive best in containers. *Fargesia rufa*, a relatively recent introduction from the mountains of Western China, makes an excellent choice. Developing into a compact arching plant, usually growing 1.5–2m tall, it is very hardy and will cope with sun or shade. It is dense but delicate in appearance with a fountain of small leaves on top of orange-green stems, and its sheaths vary from orange red to shrimpy peach colour. Maximum width in over ten years is 1.2m; although in a container this will take much longer than in the garden soil, eventually division could be necessary.

For extra height, try *Fargesia robusta* known as the walking stick bamboo. It will reach over 2m and if well looked after might grow to 3m or even more. Its culms start deep green and turn paler with age, and they are banded with paper white sheaths in summer. Maximum width in over 10 years is 1.5m, and while in a container this will take much longer than in the garden soil, again division might be needed.

A favourite amongst patio gardeners is the *Phyllostachys nigra* with its spectacular shiny black canes. They are green the first year, maturing to black thereafter. In the garden soil it can reach a height of 6m with a spread of 1.5m. Although it will grow to much less in containers, be warned –

its height makes it a tricky container plant as it will be difficult to stabilize. That does not stop it being frequently used and enjoyed. Just make sure you give it a stable container, keep it away from strong winds and remember to water it well throughout the year, especially in summer. The canes will turn blacker in full sun.

Sasa veitchii is a dwarf bamboo with broad green leaves which have an attractive bleaching of the leaf margins in autumn and winter. New growth in spring brings a crop of fresh green leaves. The culms are purple-green. It is suitable for sun or shade and would make a useful bold display beneath a taller tree. Overall height will be around 1m, but it is slow growing.

Phyllostachys nigra known as the black bamboo makes a good specimen plant for a large container in full sun. Cut out any weak growth close to ground level and remove side branches of the old culms if you want a manicured 'see through' effect.

7 SHRUBS AND CLIMBERS

Shrubs and climbers provide the backbone of the patio garden and should be considered as a long-term planting scheme. With care and attention, they will grow bigger with age and provide a framework around which to position other smaller specimens.

There are many different reasons to choose them. A white flowering shrub will light up a dark corner; a scented one will fill the patio with sweet fragrance, a glossy evergreen will add winter interest. Some, though tender, can be kept in a conservatory or greenhouse through the winter and be enjoyed for their exquisite flowers or foliage, certainly worth the effort if you are able to offer them this protection.

Hardy or tender, this permanent range of plants has something to offer in all seasons. Camellias, azaleas, rhododendrons, cytisus and early clematis will flower in spring. Spirea, roses, clematis and hydrangeas will provide early, mid and late summer colour. While eupatorium, mahonia, skimmia, and holly will offer valuable autumn and winter interest for either their ever-green foliage, flowers or berries. Bay, olive, hebes and pittosporum will offer all year round interest. (Apple trees are included in Chapter 3, while tender standard and shrub fuchsia, solanum, abutilon, heliotrope and lantana are all discussed with their bedding partners in the Chapter 2.)

For most of these long-term schemes, use a soil-based compost John Innes No 3 or a speci-fied shrub compost. The exception would be where acid-loving plants such as camellias, skim-mias and rhododendrons are planted; in this case use ericaceous compost suitable for shrubs and avoid the use of tap water which contains lime and would change the pH level of the compost to detrimental effect. It is best to consider this range of plants only if you have a water butt to store rain water.

Start the plant off in a container just a little bigger than the one you have already bought it in, and gradually move the plant on into larger pots over the years as the roots fill the available space. Beware – as the plant matures and gets bigger, it acts like a sail in the wind. So try to choose a container that sits squarely on the ground with-out rounded edges at the base; this makes it much more stable. The largest containers available at a reasonable cost are generally wooden half barrels which can be 60cm across and around 35cm deep. Don't forget to make some drainage holes, and line the base with a plastic sheet (also with drainage holes) to prevent the bottom rotting and falling apart. The shrubs may happily live in these for many years if you remember to feed and water regularly. Even so, eventually you will need to root prune the plants and re-pot using fresh compost.

SPRING FLOWERING

The hardy spring-flowering shrubs will offer extra height to the patio at a time when most of the spring colour from bulbs, primroses and wall-flowers, for example, is relatively low. The broom *Cytisus × praecox* 'Warminster' is a relatively fast growing deciduous shrub which has a mass of creamy yellow flowers in spring. Its spiky foliage and wafting form makes it an architectural 'stand

Cytisus × praecox 'Warminster' is a hardy undemanding, easy shrub to use on a sunny patio.

'Cunningham's White' is another popular choice, flowering in late spring and ideal to light up a shady corner of the patio. It grows around 1.5m high. For a smaller *Rhododendron* try one of the yakushimanum hybrids with their attractive leaves and beautiful flowers. *Rhododendron yakushimanum* 'Koichiro Wada' grows only around half a metre tall and wide, has pink buds which open white set against silvery new foliage.

EARLY, MID AND LATE SUMMER FLOWERING

Spiraea nipponica 'Snowmound' is a reliable, hardy, tough, dense, deciduous shrub with arching stems which in early summer become smothered with small white flowers. Although it likes full sun, it will still flower reasonably well in partial shade and so makes a useful choice for lighting up a dark part of the patio, beneath the end of a pergola for example. In a pot, it will eventually reach about 1.5m high and wide.

Another summer flowering shrub is the yellow jasmine *Jasminum humile* 'Revolutum' which

alone' shrub for the patio. It will probably reach about 1m or more high and wide. It will love a sunny site, and the good news is that it is drought tolerant so, although it needs moisture, it does not need constant attention. This makes it suitable for a beautifully shaped Alibaba pot where its narrow neck is restrictive for natural rainfall to water the compost.

Other attractive choices for spring would include viburnums of which there are several, both evergreen and deciduous. If you are prepared to use ericaceous soil and irrigate with rain water, then you can choose camellias and rhododendrons. They are both evergreen and the ones chosen here are both hardy and will tolerate some wind exposure. Beautiful deep rosy pink *Camellia* 'Debbie' is vigorous and very free flowering from mid to late spring. *Rhododendron*

Spiraea nipponica 'Snowmound' has arching branches bearing white flowers.

Jasminum humile 'Revolutum' is a summer-flowering hardy shrub with lightly scented flowers, which can also be grown as a short climber.

Clematis florida var. *Sieboldiana* needs winter protection, but the floral display is well worth it.

produces masses of lightly scented flowers. The flowers are borne both on old stems as well as the tips of new growth thus providing a long flowering display. It is hardy to –9 degrees C but in cold winter winds may cause some leaf loss, otherwise in sheltered areas it will be evergreen. In a pot it will grow around 1.5m high or more. It can be trained against a wall as a short climber. It is an undemanding cheery plant to have on the patio.

For a taller climber, still of the jasmine family, try *Trachelospermum jasminoides*. It will thrive in full sun or partial shade, and has neat dark green leaves to show off its small starry highly scented white flowers. It is an evergreen climber whose leaves turn deep red in winter cold. It will eventually reach 9m in ideal conditions and although it will never attain this in a pot, it might well need pruning from time to time. The best time to do this is in early spring. If drastic pruning is ever required then it is possible to reduce all shoots by two thirds, to a side shoot or flowering spur. This will encourage new shoots to break. It is one of those plants which prefers neutral rather than alkaline conditions, so where possible water with rain water otherwise, if needs must, use tap water. Water only sparingly during the winter. It is not fully hardy, so keep the container in a very sheltered spot outdoors, and fleece in very cold conditions, or safer to bring it into a greenhouse or conservatory for the winter. It can be pruned back heavily at this stage to fit the space. It will then shoot again next year and flower well.

With its white gown and vibrant purple crown, *Clematis florida* var. *sieboldiana* makes a gorgeous container plant, but it does needs winter protection in areas of frost. It is a small climber reaching up to 2m so needs support from a wooden or fine metal trellis. Delicate wirework is also excellent.

The new growth is easily trained and can be trained around the support rather than left to travel vertically. It can be planted with *Clematis* 'Pistachio' which is a single flowered cultivar from the same *C. florida* family, needing the same winter protection. They will flower from early to mid-summer. Cut back hard at the end of the flowering season to two healthy buds. *Sutera* 'Snowflake' makes an excellent under planting creating a pretty white carpet all summer long, and being perennial will last for many years. If you prefer to choose a hardy clematis for mid to late summer colour, then consider *C. purpurea plena elegans* with its double dusky blooms. Prune in late winter this time to within 15cm of soil level. It is rather taller than the florida group and will reach 2–3m high in a pot, so good support is vital. Each of these choices will provide a stunning display.

Roses are a popular choice and grow well in containers either as low shrubs or as climbers. A large deep pot or a wooden half barrel is ideal. For scent, *Rosa* 'Gertrude Jekyll' is hard to beat, flowering in early summer and then again in the early autumn. Its growth can become quite open, therefore it is helpful to use a support so that you can tie it in. For a sensational combination grow it with a mid season pink *Clematis* 'Nellie Moser'. Or try *Rosa* 'Pink Perpétue' with blue *Clematis* 'The President'. If you don't want to bother with the clematis just under plant with pink valerian *Centranthus ruber*. It will flower all summer, especially if you cut back the old flowers on a regular basis. If you don't want the hips on the rose, remove immediately after the old flowers have faded this way you will encourage new buds to form. Both these roses can be grown in pots but trained as climbers against a wall. There are very many more to choose from with a wide range of flower colour and shape and size. Look for those

BELOW: **Flower spikes on English lavender are one of the true signs of summer, heady and pungent and soft to touch.**

ABOVE: *Rosa* 'Pink Perpétue' with pink valerian *Centranthus ruber*; a central metal support has been used to tie-in the rose.

Hydrangea quercifolia 'Snowflake' makes an impressive display in a raised container so that its large flowerheads with star-shaped florets are shown off to full impact.

which are healthy and have a very good scent so that you can use them for cut flowers in the home and for cake fillings and ice creams in the kitchen. Keep them well fed and watered and they will reward you well. 'Munstead Wood' fits the description and has really deep velvety crimson blooms.

Where would the summer patio be without at least one rose and one lavender pot? They bring a touch of the cottage garden to everyone whether in the country or town, with a garden or just a balcony. Sun loving and drought tolerant, lavender makes an easy but excellent container plant. *Lavendula angustifolia*, known as the English lavender, would be my first choice in either blue, white or pink. *Lavendula* 'Munstead' has a height of around 45cm, 'Hidcote' and 'Folgate' are slightly taller at 60cm. They are all good scented compact varieties, each suited to a container. Evergreen, both foliage and flowers are highly scented, indeed the flowers can be used to flavour many cookery dishes from flapjacks, jellies, chicken casseroles and roast lamb. The flowers are highly attractive to bees. This is a sun-loving

plant which peaks in mid-summer, and if cut back immediately after flowering might produce some later flower spikes. If left uncut, the lavender might self-seed beneath the pot in paving cracks or into gravel, which would create a lovely informal carpet effect. To maintain a good shape, all lavenders benefit from an annual haircut in late summer and a further cut in the spring. French lavender *Lavendula stoechas* has a more unusual shape with rich violet bracts rather like ears. It is not as hardy as the English form and needs a sheltered spot on the patio or a greenhouse for winter protection. Its flowers smell of camphor. Give a light trim after flowering. With both types of lavenders mentioned here, never cut back into old woody stems.

By mid to late summer hydrangeas are in full flower, often continuing well into the autumn. There are many to choose from but for reliability, wow factor and size, consider *Hydrangea quercifolia* which originally comes from North America and whose leaves are lobe-shaped like the North American oak leaf. In autumn they turn a stunning russet brown. The cultivar *H.q.* 'Snowqueen' has huge trusses of pendant creamy white flowers which begin their display in mid summer and last until the autumn, adding pink tinges as they age. *H.q.* 'Snowflake' has sumptuous pendant flowers. Lifted in a container they show up so much better than when the shrub is planted in the ground. But raised, in addition, so that the container sits on a table or bench, then the display is so much more impressive. This is a hardy deciduous shrub, thriving in either sun or partial shade, which will live for many years in a container; the sunnier the spot, the more water it needs during the spring and summer.

ATTRACTIVE FOLIAGE

If you want something which has remarkably beautiful foliage in summer then consider *Acacia baileyana* 'Purpurea' which is sun loving evergreen shrub from Australia known as the purple leaved wattle. It has dainty fern like lavender green foliage with fluffy yellow flowers in late winter and early spring and all the new growth throughout the year is purple, which makes the most

delightful contrast to the older leaves. Fast growing, it will eventually reach 5m-plus in the garden but less in a container and may be pruned. Indeed, cutting back encourages new growth and prolongs the foliage contrast. Although thought to be hardy to –7°C it is safer to regard it is a tender plant and give it the shelter of a greenhouse or conservatory for the winter. If you want to plant something at the base, pale pink diascia will look charming under the blue-grey foliage of the acacia. Altogether, this is an unusual and delightful choice.

Neat, evergreen and super in flower, hebes are another favourite for containers, loving a spot in full sun or partial shade. They originate in New Zealand. They do not like winter wet, but fortunately in a container they are unlikely to have these conditions. There are very many cultivars on offer, but amongst them *Hebe* 'Caledonia' is one of the best, with its reddish purple stems, glossy leaves and violet flowers which last from mid summer to mid autumn. It makes compact

RIGHT: *Hebe* 'Caledonia' has a long flowering season and a neat habit; it is an evergreen shrub so will provide year round interest.

BELOW: *Acacia baileyana* 'Purpurea', worthy for its foliage alone; it will also produce pretty yellow flowers in early spring.

Pittosporum tenuifolium 'Tom Thumb' is a dwarf shrub with wavy dark bronze foliage; the new apple green leaves make a delightful contrast; a bronze glass mulch makes a striking addition to the mirror glazed container.

growth around 40cm high and wide. Though mainly regarded as hardy, they may have a problem with icy winter winds so keep them in the shelter of a warm house wall and choose the small-leaved types if this is a major issue.

Pittosporum, also from New Zealand, makes a good container plant with its neat, wavy, glossy leaves and striking black stems. Some have variegated cream and green foliage. Others have darker purple tones, of which possibly the best known example is *Pittosporum tenuifolium* 'Tom Thumb', a dwarf variety reaching only around 45–60cm high in a pot. Its new growth is light green which makes a delightful contrast. It has fragrant flowers in late spring and early summer, although these are not reliably forthcoming. Primarily it is grown for its attractive foliage and neat form. Pittosporum likes a position in full sun; in winter however offer it a sheltered spot, and in severe weather take it into the greenhouse. *P. t.* 'Victoria' has pale silvery leaves edged white, and interestingly the leaves become tinged dark

The bronze cordyline is planted with mounds of summer bedding including yellow
Sanvitalia and blue lobelia.

purple in winter. It is considered a hardy variety but still take care in frosty weather. Any of the darker leaved types look great in metallic, black or mirror containers. Plant them as specimen shrubs just on their own with a topping of grit, or for a more modern twist add coloured stones or glass.

If you want to bring a tropical look to your patio, then try growing *Cordyline australis*. It is a palm-like tree which in its native New Zealand can grow 20m tall. It will never make that height in a container, of course; indeed just a few metres would be the exception. It is the strong sword-like leaves which give it its characteristic shape and make it such a striking plant. There are various cultivars available, with varying coloured foliage, some with green and red stripes, some with pink in the leaf such as 'Pink Stripe' and some all bronze such as 'Red Star' or 'Torbay Red'. Once they have grown a trunk, they are regarded as being hardy down to about −9°C, but they will not like winter wet, and certainly not winter snow. The simplest way to cope is just to move them into a dry site whilst snowy weather persists or cover with a fleece to keep their centres drier.

If planted in a sumptuous beehive pot, then something extra special can be added. There is ample space around the base of the cordyline trunk to create an exciting partnership. Bronze, blue and yellow sit well together, and blue lobelia plus creeping yellow *Sanvitalia speciosa* 'Aztec Gold' makes a good understorey. However for a longer-term solution try yellow violas for late spring with the dainty grass *Stipa tenuissima* planted between them. In summer orange *Lotus berthelotii* can replace the violas and provide long trails of feathery silver foliage hugging the sides of the container. The grasses will grow quickly, turning from green to gold as they flower and mature, billowing out to echo the shape of the beehive pot, catching the sun as they are tossed and swayed in the summer breezes. This beehive pot has a false plastic bowl which fits snugly inside the top, and it is here that the cordyline is planted, making winter treatment much easier because it can simply be lifted out and placed in a dry sheltered place if snow or very cold winds threaten. A similar pot with ivies can be used to

Wispy *Stipa tenuissima* offers a strong contrast to the sword-like leaves of the cordyline in this alternative scheme.

replace it. In early autumn remove and pot up the lotus and give winter protection so that you can plant it out again next year. The grasses are perennial and should survive. Trim them hard back in late winter.

For structural all year round container interest try evergreen bay *Laurus nobilis* or olive *Olea europaea*. They both make handsome specimens and make a relative easy container gardening plant, often seen beside a doorway or a flight of steps. Both can be bought either very small or large; indeed a bay can be purchased with a double spiral trunk if you are prepared to pay the price. They are both relatively hardy, but during the winter keep them in a sunny sheltered site – close to the house wall or beside a sunny doorway is ideal – and in very severe weather take them into a greenhouse or conservatory.

Bay will bloom in early spring with small yellowish green flowers. Its leaves can be used as a herb in the kitchen, added (then discarded) to flavour many fish dishes, soups and casseroles as well as sweeter delicacies. Be warned, a mature tree in open ground can grow to 8m, so although you might purchase a beautifully trimmed cone or ball, it will eventually grow out of shape. Pruning is straightforward, however – do it twice each year, first in mid spring and again in late summer; if you want a complete change or drastic pruning, always do it mid spring as this gives the plant chance to put on plenty of dense new growth during the summer. Use trimmings as a store of dried bay leaves for the kitchen.

In recent years olive trees have become a popular choice for pots on a sheltered patio or balcony. They are hardier than once thought, often surviving frost and snow in the olive groves in Croatia and northern Spain, for example.

Known as the incense bush, *Eupatorium ligustrinum* produces very welcome flowers in late summer and early autumn.

However, as a younger plant, it will be more susceptible to severe weather, so take extra care for the first few years.

The fragrant creamy white flowers appear in summer and are largely wind pollinated. For a harvest to occur, the tree must have dry weather at flowering time. *Olea europaea* 'Picual' is probably one of the most reliable to fruit, and is self-fertile so one tree is sufficient for a crop. But in the UK, summers are relatively cool and short compared with the Mediterranean climate, and ripening will take a long time. So it is probably best to think of the olive crop as a bonus, and just enjoy the beautiful shape and beautiful grey-green colour of the leaves.

A beautiful terracotta pot would make an ideal home, but then a rusty metal container would look good as well. Or try a shiny glazed pot. If you place it in a strategic position by a door, maybe the door could be painted a sympathetic colour. In open ideal conditions an olive tree can grow to 10m or more. Although it will never reach this in a container, it does cope well with being pruned, which is generally done in late February to March.

AUTUMN AND WINTER APPEAL

An unusual shrub to try in a pot is *Eupatorium ligustrinum*. Again it is evergreen, this time from Mexico. The highlight comes in late summer and early autumn when its scented white flowers appear, attractive to bees and butterflies. Eventually it might reach over 1m in height and width in the pot. It can withstand temperatures down to –5°C, but after that would suffer. To be on the safe side, treat as frost hardy, keep it on the dry side during the winter and offer protection if temperatures fall below freezing.

For all year round interest, but with special appeal in the colder months, mahonia and holly are two very hardy evergreen plants which make excellent specimens for the winter patio, to frame a doorway or simply place by the back door. They are easy to site, in sun, partial shade or even full shade; the sunnier the spot the earlier in the autumn the mahonia will flower.

There are several mahonias to choose from, including *Mahonia* × *media* 'Charity', 'Winter Sun' and 'Lionel Fortescue'. They are all similar architectural plants with large pinnate leaves and a strongly branched structure. Pretty little yellow flowers emerge on long spikes from autumn through to late winter. Each tiny flower looks like a miniature daffodil, but smells like lily of the valley – the perfect reason to enjoy it by your doorway. If you have another plant you prefer for scent in late spring or summer then just swap the pots around. That's the joy of container gardening.

In a large container both mahonia and holly will eventually grow around 2m tall. They are not thirsty plants, indeed they are content with 'occasional' rather than too much watering, and this is especially true of the winter months.

Holly is undemanding, like the mahonia. They respond well to pruning and so can be shaped quite easily. Either grow as a clipped cylinder or as a standard lollipop. They can then be enjoyed as a pair. To retain the shape a light clipping should be done in June and again at the end of August. If you forget to do this, don't worry, more drastic pruning can still be done with no long-term damage; the holly will just take a couple of seasons to bush out again.

The variegated holly *Ilex aquifolium* 'Argentea Marginata' is a female holly, perfect for the winter garden with its shiny red berries, and it also looks good in late spring and early summer when it has its distinctive soft new leaves with pink tinges. A female holly will need a male in the wider vicinity in order to berry, so if you are unsure about this buy *Ilex* 'J.C. Van Tol' which is self-fertile.

This pair of variegated holly *Ilex aquifolium* 'Argentea Marginata' have been planted in large pots. In late spring and early summer its distinctive soft new leaves with pink tinges are a perfect accompaniment to *Rosa* 'Gertrude Jekyll' on the left and *Clematis montana* 'Broughton Star' on the right.

8 PLANTING GUIDE AND AFTERCARE RECIPES

Planting Guide

1. Start with a clean container.
2. Check there is an adequate drainage hole(s) at the base.
3. (Optional) In the case of unglazed terracotta or unvarnished wooden containers, line the sides and base of the container with black plastic (bin liner or a cut-up compost bag) to prevent water loss. This will keep the container drier from the inside and is an aid to avoid frost damage in terracotta and to prevent rot in wood. Don't forget to make extra drainage hole(s) in the plastic to coincide with those underneath.
4. Cover the base with at least 2.5cm of drainage material; you can use more if your container is deep. Use broken crocks or broken poly-styrene, which is light.
5. (Optional) Add a plant membrane over the drainage material to prevent the soil washing out and roots clogging the drainage hole.
6. Fill with compost mixed with a slow-release pelleted feed. Select the compost to suit your plants:
   Soil-based for bulbs, shrubs and all long-term work; for succulents add extra grit.
   Ericaceous for acid loving plants.
   Multi-purpose for spring and summer work including bedding plants and vegetables; you might add water retaining crystals before planting.
7. Plant your choice of seasonal colour, succulents, herbaceous plants or vegetables. The top of the compost in all cases should be at least 2.5cm below the rim of the container.

For bulbs, bring the compost layer up to allow for the 'three times the depth of the bulbs' rule, and then add more compost on top.

For shrubs, bring the compost layer up to allow for the shrub to be planted at the same depth as the pot in which it is growing. Soak the plant for two hours beforehand, remove the plant from the pot and add more compost to fill the sides of the container.

8. Water well. Firm down the plants and add more compost if necessary, bringing level to within 2.5cm of rim. This small gap will prevent the compost being washed away and making a mess down the sides of the container. It also allows space for a mulch.
9. (Optional) Add mulch or, if planting a single shrub or single stem succulent, add a mulching mat and then mulch.

Aftercare

1. Keep the compost moist whilst the plants are actively in growth; water daily if necessary.
2. Apply liquid feed regularly. If a slow-release pelleted feed has already been added, this will suffice for the first season. Thereafter apply a liquid feed.
3. Deadhead pelargoniums, fuchsias, begonias, sweet peas and other bedding plants as often as possible, at least once a week. (Obviously avoid this with vegetables or you will have no crop!)
   In the autumn take precautions for all those containers which include non-hardy plants.
4. In spring apply a multi-purpose granular fertilizer at soil level, avoiding foliage, to second season pots and any older ones; but leave succulents alone.

RECIPES

Simple Summer Basket, Wall Pot or Window Box with Bedding Plants

Container: Small to medium; wicker or painted basket 25cm long × 20cm wide and only 10cm deep

Season: Plant late spring and keep in greenhouse or outdoors in early summer

Ingredients (using tender plants)
2   *Diascia barberae* 'Blackthorn Apricot'
1   *Brachyscome iberidifolia* also known as the blue swan river daisy
Compost: multi-purpose compost
Water gel crystals
Drainage such as light polystyrene
Black lining for basket

Planting Guide
1. Wicker baskets will have good drainage, but wooden ones might need some holes drilled; take action as necessary.
2. Line the basket with a black plastic lining (e.g. bin liner).
3. Cut several small slits into the plastic lining to allow drainage.
4. Add compost bringing it to within 2.5cm of the rim of the basket.
5. Add water gel crystals and a scattering of slow-release fertilizer according to instructions on the packet. Mix both very thoroughly.
6. Plant the brachyscome in the middle of the container with the diascias on either side.
7. Water well, firm in the plants.

Aftercare
Keep compost moist throughout the summer; water at soil level, daily if necessary.

Deadhead to encourage further flowering.

For a more radical treatment at the turn from mid to late summer (early August is ideal), cut off all the top growth, leaving about 8cm of growth. Then apply a liquid feed to promote fresh growth. The basket will come into full growth again during late summer and through the autumn. Protect from frost on nights when these occur but otherwise continue to enjoy until early winter.

Discard all contents and start again next year.

A basket of pink diascia and brachyscome.

You can give the arrangement a radical haircut in mid to late summer.

Petunia Surfinia[PBR] and scaevola in hanging basket.

Easy Hanging Basket with Summer Bedding Plants

Container: Medium to large; 36cm diameter lined wicker hanging basket with suitable bracket

Season: Plant late spring and keep in greenhouse or outdoors in early summer

Ingredients (using tender plants)

1   *Petunia* 'Surfinia Hot Red'[PBR]
1   *Petunia* 'Surfinia Sky Blue'[PBR]
1   *Scaevola aemula* 'Zig Zag'
1   *Scaevola aemula* 'Blue Wonder'

Compost: multi-purpose compost
Water-retaining crystals
Drainage, such as light polystyrene

Planting Guide

1. Cut several small slits into the plastic lining at the base of the hanging basket.
2. Add compost bringing it to within 2.5cm of the rim of the basket. Add water gel crystals and a scattering of slow-release fertilizer according to instructions on the packet. (Water-retaining crystals can either be added to water before mixing them with the compost, or just added dry.) Mix both very thoroughly.
3. Plant a petunia and then a scaevola at equal intervals around the edge of the basket.
4. Water well, firm in the plants and hang basket in sun or partial shade.

Aftercare

Keep compost moist throughout the summer; water at soil level, daily if necessary.

By late summer start giving an additional fortnightly liquid feed.

There is no need to deadhead any of these flowers.

Before the first frosts, remove basket from the bracket. You can either discard all contents, or remove and discard the petunias and overwinter the scaevolas in a frost-free greenhouse so that they can be saved for use the following summer.

Mix water-retaining crystals thoroughly with compost before planting.

Hanging Basket with Herbaceous Plants

Container: Medium to large; 36cm diameter lined wicker hanging basket with suitable bracket.
Plant: Spring or early summer

Ingredients (all hardy)

1 *Hosta* 'Red October' (alternatively plant 'Golden Tiara' or 'Fire and Ice')
3 *Lysimachia nummularia* 'Aurea', Golden Creeping Jenny
4 *Mimulus hybridus* monkey flower, either red or burgundy, pink, cream or whatever you like best

Compost: John Innes No 2 or a multi-purpose compost
Long-term slow-release fertilizer
Drainage such as light polystyrene

Planting Guide

1. Cut several small slits into the plastic lining at the base of the hanging basket.
2. Add 2.5cm of drainage material and then add 10cm of compost.
3. Add a scattering of slow-release fertilizer according to instructions on the packet.
4. Plant the hosta in the centre of the basket with the top of the roots 2.5cm below the rim.
5. Arrange the three creeping jenny plants around the edge so that the trails will fall over the front and sides, with two mimulus on either side of the hosta, front and back.

6. Fill in the gaps with compost bringing level to within 2.5cm of rim.
7. Water well and hang basket in partial shade.

Aftercare

Keep compost moist throughout the spring and especially summer, autumn and winter, but never water in frosty weather.

Make sure the hosta leaves do not touch the wall at the back; if so they will act as a system for slugs and snails which will then harm the hosta foliage.

Deadhead the mimulus flowers in early summer to promote further flowering; eventually leave some to self-seed in the basket for the following year.

Do not deadhead the hosta flowers on their tall red stems, but enjoy the seedheads which are also tinged with red.

In autumn cut off dead hosta leaves, trim back the creeping jenny close to soil level and remove old mimulus leaving any seedlings in place; leave basket suspended so that it is away from slugs and snails.

Each spring thereafter apply a slow-release fertilizer at soil level, avoiding any emerging foliage.

Leave basket on bracket, even in winter, so that slugs and snails don't invade.

Hostas, golden creeping jenny and mimulus hanging basket.

MICRO GARDENING

Eggs with Succulents

Containers: Large eggs or any small containers
    such as mini terracotta pots
Season: Plant anytime
Site: Sunny position

Even an eggshell can be used as a container.

Ingredients

Small hardy succulents – either buy or gather a
selection from existing plants; these might
include various houseleeks *Sempervivum*, or
you might choose stonecrops such as *Sedum
rupestre* 'Angelina', *Sedum acre* 'aureum', or
Sedum spathulifolium 'Cape Blanco'.
Tender succulents – you might use plants which
will need winter protection, such as *Echeveria
elegans*.

Compost: Multi-purpose or soil-based John Innes
    No 2
Drainage such as broken pots or polystyrene

Planting Guide

1. If using eggs, carefully remove tops of large
hard-boiled eggs along with contents.
2. Make a hole at the base of each empty shell
with a pin.
3. Add a few teaspoons of the compost to fill the
egg.
4. Plant a small succulent in the top and gently
water.
5. Place egg containers on an egg stand or cupcake stand and keep outside in a sunny place.

Aftercare

These plants do not need much water, but to
keep compost moist use a teapot or milk jug
to water them.
When the succulents grow on and fill the top of
the egg, sink the eggs in a bowl of water to
moisten the compost.
After six or nine months you might need to
replant, at which stage you may be able to
remove some of the offsets growing around
the sides of the main plant.
If using tender succulents such as echeveria, bring
indoors for the winter and enjoy as houseplants.

**Hardy
sempervivum in
a micro garden.**

SOWING VEGETABLES FROM SEED

Hardy: Sow Direct in Container (e.g. peas)

Peas resent root disturbance if transplanted from seed tray to permanent placement. Sow direct from early to late spring, preferably in succession to ensure a succession of cropping. 'Sugar Snow Green' is a dwarf, flat, broad-podded mangetout type of pea. The pods can be eaten raw or lightly cooked and are a good source of vitamins A and C, iron and potassium.

Container: Any large container, deep bucket or
    even a lined wicker hanging basket
Season: Sow early to late spring outdoors
Site: Sunny position

Ingredients
10 Pea 'Sugar Snow Green' seeds
1   Mentha spicata mint (Optional)
Compost: Multi-purpose
Drainage such as broken pots or polystyrene

Planting Guide
1. Sow the seeds 2.5cm deep, 20cm apart, in pairs.

RIGHT: **Pea 'Sugar Snow Green', a mangetout type of peas best eaten whole, before the pods are swollen.**

BELOW: **Pea 'Sugar Snow Green' sown direct into a container with a water reservoir.**

2. Once germination has occurred, usually after 7 to 10 days, then remove the weaker seedlings; this helps to ensure loss through vermin or bird damage.
3. (Optional) Plant the mint at the side nearest the sun.
4. This pea grows to around 30cm high and needs the support of canes, sticks or trellis; in a hanging basket you can allow it to flop.

Aftercare
Keep the container moist, topping up through
    the reservoir pipe.
Crop the mint as needed.
Crop the peas as soon as the small pods begin to
    form; the more you pick, the more will be
    produced.
After the crop has finished, cut down and
    compost the pea stems, and let the mint flour-
    ish; it will grow quickly and provide good
    material for divisions the following year.

Tender: Sow and Transplant to Container (e.g. tomatoes)

Tender vegetables can be sown direct into outdoor containers after risk of frost, but by sowing them earlier into a seed tray, in a warm greenhouse or on a window sill, the germination time will be quicker, and the plants will be ready to harvest earlier. This also enables you to grow plants which need a long growing season. Runner beans, French beans, courgettes, tomatoes, cucumbers, aubergines and sweetcorn can all benefit from this treatment.

Home-grown tomatoes are wonderful for containers, especially if you choose the smaller fruiting tumbling varieties which need no support. Tomato 'Gartenperle' is a very good old German heirloom variety, while tomatoes 'Balconi Red' and 'Balconi Yellow' are also excellent and fun to grow with their contrasting coloured fruit. There is no need to remove sideshoots of any of these. 'Gartenperle' crops within 100 days of sowing, while the other two are quicker, taking seventy days. They can also be kept in the greenhouse all summer where they will crop sooner and longer.

Container: Hanging basket, window box, tub, bucket or pot
Season: Sow indoors early to mid spring
Site: Sunny position

Ingredients
Tomato 'Gartenperle' seeds (one plant per 30cm basket, two plants in a 41cm basket)
(Optional) Sweet Basil *Ocimum basilicum* seedlings (could be a pot from the supermarket)
Compost: Seed compost, and then multi-purpose compost
Water-retaining crystals
Drainage such as broken pots or polystyrene

Planting Guide
1. Prepare seed tray by filling with damp seed compost.
2. Sow the seeds thinly on surface of the seed compost.

Pick the strongest seedlings from the seed tray.

Plant individually in 8cm pots.

3. Cover seeds with a very thin layer 6mm deep of vermiculite.
4. Place in a propagator at 18–20°C until germination has occurred, usually after seven to fourteen days. They will also germinate in the greenhouse without extra heat, although germination might take longer; it can help to cover with a plastic bag to retain moist conditions. Remove the bag after germination.
5. Transplant seedlings when large enough to handle and when a good root system has begun to form.
6. Plant each seedling into an 8cm pot using a multi-purpose compost.
7. In late spring, when the plants are around 15cm or more high, plant in permanent hanging baskets, window boxes or containers.

This two-tier hanging basket of tomatoes and basil is just outside the kitchen door.

Use drainage material covered with a multi-purpose compost mixed with water-retaining crystals. For a 30cm diameter basket only one plant is needed. In this larger double tiered basket, two tomatoes have been planted in each basket.

8. The plants need to be hardened off gradually for a week or two to cope with outdoor temperatures, so move outside during the daytime but bring them back into the greenhouse for the evening and night time. Only leave outside permanently once all risk of frost has passed. Choose a sunny spot.

9. (Optional) In early summer add basil in the middle of each basket. You can plant a whole pack or split the seedlings into small groups.

They will help to ward off whitefly but basil also makes a delicious addition to any tomato dishes.

Aftercare

Keep the container moist, watering daily if necessary; always water at soil level avoiding excess water on any leaves or fruit.

Feed with a liquid tomato fertilizer once a week, starting when the first fruits begin to form.

This tomato is a bush variety known as a tumbler, which naturally trails and needs no support, stopping or side shooting.

Harvest tomatoes mid summer to mid autumn (100 days from sowing to picking). Crop basil any time and also enjoy the tasty flowers.

RIGHT: **Bulbs are planted at three times their depth.**

A long-term pot of daffodils in mid spring.

BULBS

Bulbs should be planted in a soil-based compost such as John Innes No 2. Bulbs are planted 'nose' upwards with roots at the bottom. They are planted at three times their depth, so a tulip bulb which might be 5cm high would be planted with its base 15cm below soil level and its nose 10cm below soil level. Therefore the deeper the bulb, the deeper the pot will need to be. Please be aware that both tulips and daffodils are available as tall or dwarf, with relatively large or small bulbs. Space the bulbs allowing 5cm or more between bulbs, but they can be planted closer so long as they do not touch either each other or the sides of the container.

For a two-tier container, when planting two sorts of bulbs, plant the larger one below, cover with a little compost and then plant the smaller bulbs in between the shoulders of the deeper ones. Cover with compost, add violas or pansies – the bulbs will push their way through any roots formed on these plants. However, if planting a shrub, then plant the bulbs around the base of the shrub rather than beneath it as the root system will be much denser. Grit or shell can then be added as a mulch. The example in the photo on page 127 shows a small terracotta pot 20cm wide, 23cm deep with a two-tier planting using five *Narcissus* 'Hawera' and eight *Muscari latifolium* which will then flower together in mid to late spring. *Narcissus* 'Bellsong' or 'Segovia' could have been used instead of 'Hawera'.

ABOVE LEFT: **Drainage material at the base of the pot.**

ABOVE RIGHT: **Five *Narcissus* 'Hawera' spaced so they touch neither each other nor the sides of the pot.**

RIGHT: **Plant eight smaller *Muscari latifolium* between the shoulders of the deeper bulbs.**

Long-term Daffodil Pot

Container: Deep, medium sized, such as this terracotta pot 45cm wide by 35cm deep
Season: Plant in autumn
Site: Sunny or partially shaded position

Ingredients: (all hardy)
10 Daffodil *Narcissus* 'Romance'
3   variegated London pride *Saxifraga* × *urbium* 'Aureopunctata' (it will establish to cover the pot in two seasons)

Compost: John Innes No 2
Drainage such as broken pots or polystyrene
Membrane over drainage material (optional)

Planting Guide
1. Place 5cm drainage at the bottom of the pot and cover with (optional) plant membrane or sacking over the top to protect roots and soil from clogging drainage hole.
2. Cover with 10cm of compost (or more depending on depth of container); you are aiming to plant the bulbs three times their depth.

Deadhead daffodils after flowering.

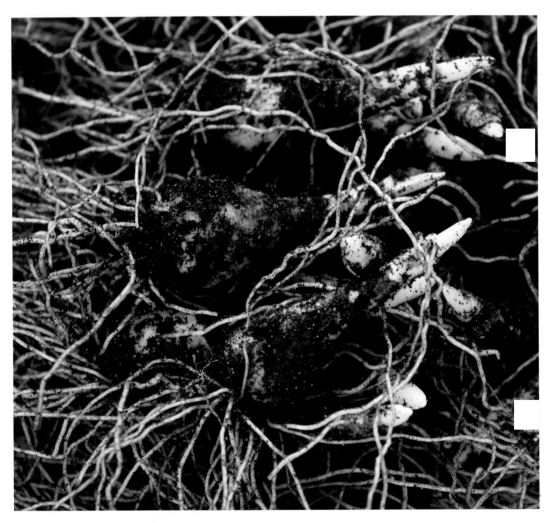

ABOVE: Contents of the daffodil pot have been removed and the bulbs carefully separated.

LEFT: The bulbs have been replanted in one medium-sized pot.

3. Place the daffodil bulbs, snout upwards, in a ring allowing 5cm or more between bulbs.
4. Cover with compost bringing level to within 2.5cm of rim.
5. Plant the three London pride plants around the edge of the pot.
6. Water well.

Aftercare (Year 1, 2 and 3)

Keep compost moist throughout the autumn, winter and spring, but never water in frosty weather.

Give a liquid feed in mid spring to encourage the bulbs to replenish their food reserves for next year's flower display.

Deadhead daffodils to prevent seedheads forming.

Six weeks after the daffodils have finished flowering their leaves will turn yellow and wither; by then the London Pride flowers are over. Remove the daffodil leaves and cut off the London pride flower stems, leaving a tidy pot with just a neat frill of evergreen London pride.

Aftercare (Year 3 Early Autumn)

Carefully empty contents of pot and gently ease apart the daffodils which by now will have multiplied. Wash the pot.

Use drainage material, plant membrane (optional) and fresh compost as above, then plant individual bulbs, ten to a container.

You will now have surplus to plant in other containers (plant eight in a medium pot or ten if using a larger size pot) or in the garden.

Top up with soil.

Divide the London pride, replanting three plants to each pot. Top with a gritty mulch.

Water well and place pots in a sunny or partially shaded position.

Container with Tulips (one season only)

Container: Deep, medium-sized, such as this blue glazed pot 35cm wide × 35cm deep
Season: Plant autumn
Site: Sunny position

Ingredients (all hardy)

6   *Tulipa* 'Negrita' (purple)
6   *Tulipa* 'Angelique' (pink)
3   pale blue pansies (could use forget-me-nots or wallflowers).

Compost: John Innes No 2
Drainage such as broken pots or polystyrene

Planting Guide

1. Place 5cm drainage at the bottom of the pot.
2. Cover with 10cm of compost (or more depending on depth of container); you are aiming to plant the bulbs three times their depth.
3. Space the tulip bulbs alternately, snout upwards, in two rings allowing 5cm or more between bulbs.
4. Cover with compost bringing level to within 2.5cm of rim.

Deadhead pansies to encourage further flowering.

5. Plant the three pansies around the edge of the pot. Add a grit mulch (optional).
6. Water well and put pot in a sunny position.

Aftercare

Keep compost moist throughout the autumn, winter and spring, but never water in frosty weather.

Give a liquid feed in mid spring to encourage the pansies into greater flower production.

Deadhead pansies to encourage further flowering.

Discard contents in late spring and replant pot with summer colour.

GRASSES

Container with Deciduous Grasses

Container: Small to medium; this is a blue glazed pot 30cm wide by 30cm deep
Season: Plant spring or summer

Japanese blood grass becomes more intense with a lot of sun.

Ingredients (relatively slow growing and frost hardy plants)

1 *Imperata cylindrica* 'Rubra', known as Japanese blood grass, which is frost hardy

Compost John Innes No 2
Drainage such as broken pots or polystyrene
Membrane over drainage material

Planting Guide

1. Place 5cm drainage at the bottom of the pot with (optional) plant membrane or sacking over the top to prevent roots and soil from clogging drainage hole.
2. Cover with 10cm of compost or more depending on depth of container. Add a scattering of slow-release fertilizer and mix well.
3. Plant the grass in the middle, with the top of the roots 2.5cm below the rim of the pot.
4. Fill in the gaps with more compost, bringing level to within 2.5cm of rim.
5. Mulch direct with horticultural grit or broken shells, which will allow new shoots to grow; avoid top mulching mat as this grass will grow to fill the pot and needs the space to expand.
6. Water well and put pot in sun or partial shade; the sunnier the site the better the colouring.

Aftercare

Keep compost moist throughout the autumn, spring and especially summer.

In frosty weather take the pot into a greenhouse until milder weather returns. During these cold spells, deliberately keep compost on the dry side.

In late winter cut off all top growth back to within 8–10cm of soil level.

Apply a multi-purpose granular fertilizer in early spring.

After three years, in spring move into a larger pot; or to keep in same pot, remove and cut off the lower third of roots, add fresh compost and pot up into the same pot as before.

NB. For fully hardy grasses, there is no need for greenhouse protection. For more vigorous grasses, especially deciduous ones such as miscanthus and panicum, an annual potting is preferable as they grow so fast and exhaust the soil. Repot in late winter after cutting back. For those potted annually a slow-release fertilizer can be mixed in with the compost.

Before new growth begins, cut off and remove all top growth.

Container with Evergreen Grasses

Container: Small to medium; this is a small glazed pot 30cm wide by 30cm deep
Season: Plant spring or summer

Ingredients (hardy)
1   *Carex* 'Evergold'

Compost: John Innes No 2
Drainage such as broken pots or polystyrene
Membrane over drainage material

Planting Guide
1. Place 5cm drainage at the bottom of the pot with (optional) plant membrane or sacking over the top to prevent roots and soil from clogging drainage hole.
2. Cover with 10cm of compost or more depending on depth of container. Add a scattering of slow-release fertilizer and mix well.
3. Plant the grass with the top of the roots 5cm below the rim of the pot.
4. Fill in the gaps with more compost, bringing level to within 2.5cm of rim.
5. Mulch direct with horticultural grit or broken shells which will allow new shoots to grow. Avoid top mulching mat as this grass will grow to fill the pot and needs the space to expand.
6. Water well and put pot in sun or partial shade.

Aftercare
Keep compost moist throughout the autumn, winter, spring and especially summer, but never water in frosty weather.
In late spring rake out any dead leaves, or trim dead ends. If grass is very untidy, cut back to 8–10cm and it will soon start to re-grow.
Apply a multi-purpose granular fertilizer in spring and or give a liquid feed in early summer.
After three years, in spring move into a larger pot; or to keep in same pot, remove and cut off the lower third of roots, add fresh compost and pot up into the same pot as before.

NB In frosty weather, take any tender evergreens into a greenhouse until milder weather returns. During these cold spells, deliberately keep compost on the dry side.

Carex 'Evergold', in the middle of winter, keeps remarkably tidy.

ABOVE: *Pittosporum tenuifolium* 'Tom Thumb', with decorative material on top of the membrane collar.

LEFT: Shape a collar of membrane to fit top of pot, with centre circle removed and a slit made across the collar for ease of fitting round the shrub.

SHRUBS

Container with Single-Stemmed Shrub plus Decorative Mulch

Container: Small to medium sized deep container. Choose size just a little bigger than the plastic pot in which the shrub is already planted, allowing 5cm drainage and 2.5cm for top gap. This is a mirror-glazed pot 28cm wide × 25cm deep

Season: Plant spring or summer

Site: Sunny position

Ingredients (frost hardy)

1 *Pittosporum tenuifolium* 'Tom Thumb'

Compost: John Innes No 3

Drainage such as broken pots or polystyrene

Membrane to cover drainage material at base of pot, and also used as a collar under mulch at top of pot

Mulch such as horticultural grit, bark, broken shells, glass ornamental mulch; choose your mulch to match plant or pot

Planting Guide

1. Place 5cm drainage at the bottom of the pot with (optional) plant membrane or sacking over the top to prevent roots and soil from clogging drainage hole.
2. Add 5cm of compost or more depending on depth of container.
3. Plant the shrub with the top of the roots 2.5cm below the rim of the pot.
4. Fill in the gaps with more compost, bringing level to within 2.5cm of rim.
5. Water well.
6. Cut out collar from a mulch mat with central hole for stems; place collar around the base of the shrub to help to prevent the mulch sinking into the soil and getting dirty.
7. Add the layer of mulch.

Aftercare

Keep compost moist throughout the autumn, winter and spring, but never water in frosty weather.

Unless hardy, in frosty weather take the pot into a greenhouse until milder weather returns; during these cold spells, deliberately keep compost on the dry side.

In spring remove decorative stones and mulch mat, apply a multi-purpose granular fertilizer, then replace mat and stones.

After three years repot in early summer into a slightly larger pot.

NB. For fully hardy shrubs, there is no need for greenhouse protection.

9 YEAR ROUND CALENDAR

MID TO LATE WINTER

Choose from seed catalogues and garden centres the seeds you would like to buy for this year's containers, including annual ornamental grasses, colourful nasturtiums, pot marigolds and sunflowers, herbs such as dill, caraway and parsley; vegetables such as peas, beans, carrots, beetroot, courgettes and tomatoes, plus seed potatoes. You will also find a wide variety of dry bulbs including begonias, lilies, cannas, eucomis and nerines.

Indoors

If outdoor temperatures are above freezing, open up the greenhouse for an hour or so on sunny days to increase ventilation. Keep temperatures frost free at night-time.

Don't be tempted to water your pots very much at all. Once or twice in the whole season from mid autumn to late winter might well be sufficient. Certainly do not water in frosty conditions, however tempting it may be on a sunny winter's day when the greenhouse is nice and warm; this is because sunny days mean very cold nights.

Outdoors

Don't be tempted to water your pots except to maintain a 'just moist' scenario. Window boxes might get dry if in the rain shadow of a building, so check from time to time, but never water in frosty conditions.

Protect any pots with frost-hardy plants with bubble wrap or fleece in severe weather. In late winter, cut back deciduous grasses to within 10cm of soil level.

OPPOSITE: **Tulips and pansies in all their glory.**

Now is the time to enjoy snowdrops and winter flowering aconites as well as very early daffodils, crocus, violas, hellebores, ivies and cornus.

SPRING

Early Spring

Indoors

Sow those seeds which have a long germination period or those that have a long growing period until they flower or fruit. You can start many off now, but the earlier you begin the longer you will have to hold tender varieties in the confines of your greenhouse before the last frosts have disappeared.

Apply a slow-release general fertilizer to long-term pots.

From early to mid spring, begin to water over-wintered plants which are showing signs of new shoots. Don't be tempted to overwater at this stage.

Outdoors

Sow seeds of hardy annuals such as sweet peas, garden peas and *Lagurus ovatus* the bunny tail grass. Plant lily bulbs in pots.

Apply a slow-release general fertilizer to long-term pots.

Enjoy dwarf daffodils, early tulips, hyacinths, crocus, primroses, violets, violas, hellebores, and ivies.

Mid Spring

Indoors

Sow tender seeds now so that they are sturdy for planting out towards the end of spring. This is the busiest sowing period. Plant begonia tubers, eucomis, cannas and dahlias. Divide cannas.

From early to mid spring, begin to water overwintered plants which are showing signs of new shoots. Don't be tempted to overwater at this stage.

Outdoors

Sow seeds of hardy annuals such as sweet peas, garden peas, *Calendula officinalis* and *Lagurus ovatus* the bunny tail grass.

For long-term pots of shrubs, grasses and lilies remove any weeds, and add a shallow layer of fresh compost mixed with a general purpose fertilizer.

Watch out for signs of slug and snail damage, vine weevil beetles, lily beetles on the fritillarias, and Solomon's seal sawfly, and act as necessary.

Enjoy daffodils, tulips, fritillarias, grape hyacinths, *leucojum aestivum*, primroses, violets, violas, bellis daisies, pansies and wallflowers.

Late Spring

Indoors

You can still sow tender seeds indoors. It is warmer now so any seed planted will be quicker to germinate and grow on.

Transplant your newly germinated seeds of courgettes, beans and tomatoes into 8cm pots and then again into their summer baskets and containers.

Make up your new containers with begonias and cannas.

Gradually harden off young plants during the daytime, bringing them back to the greenhouse at night-time so that they become accustomed to outdoor temperatures. Once all risk of frost has passed you can leave them outside all the time, but beware early summer evenings can be cold. Keep cannas in the greenhouse until well into early summer.

Open up the greenhouse for several hours on sunny days to increase ventilation. Keep temperatures frost free at night-time.

By late spring as temperatures rise the days grow longer and the plants begin to put on growth in earnest; then watering will be very important (except for succulents, which should be kept on the dry side). Always water at soil level

to avoid run-off. Water in the early morning or evening. Avoid watering when sun is shining on leaves to avoid scorch; this is a particular problem with begonias.

Watch out for signs of damage from slugs and snails and vine weevils, and act as necessary.

Outdoors

Sow tender seeds which will germinate after the risk of frost has passed (cover seedlings with newspaper if frost does threaten). It is warmer now so any seed planted will be quicker to germinate and grow on.

Make sure your pots are kept moist; water as necessary.

Deadhead pansies, violas and daffodils.

Apply a spring liquid feed to any pots with bedding and to any pots of bulbs which you have overwintered.

Tidy evergreen grasses or cut back to within 10cm of soil level.

Pinch out tops of sweet pea plants when they are 10cm high to encourage lateral shoots.

Watch out for signs of slug and snail damage, vine weevil beetles, lily beetles on the fritillarias, and Solomon's seal sawfly, and act as necessary.

Enjoy tulips, violas, bellis daisies, forget-me-nots, pansies, wallflowers, dicentra, Solomon's seal, sweet woodruff, hostas, new fern fronds, and shrubs such as cytisus.

SUMMER

Early Summer

There is still time to make up summer containers with bedding plants. Plant outside.

Move cannas outside once temperatures have really warmed up both in the daytime and during the nights.

Make sure your pots are kept moist and water as necessary (succulents should be kept on the dry side). Always water at soil level to avoid run-off. Water in the early morning or evening. Avoid watering when sun is shining on leaves, otherwise they will scorch, particularly with begonias.

Deadhead regularly.

Begin to give a fortnightly liquid feed to all long-term summer flowering containers which have been overwintered.

Watch out for signs of slug and snail damage, vine weevil beetles, lily beetles on emerging lilies, and Solomon's seal sawfly, greenfly and blackfly and act as necessary.

Enjoy shrubs such as spiraea, early flowering grasses, herbaceous plants including heucheras, foxgloves, hostas, ferns, mimulus and early flowering tender bedding plants.

Harvest salad leaves, early peas and herb leaves.

Mid Summer

Make sure your pots are kept moist and water as necessary (succulents should be kept on the dry side). Always water at soil level to avoid run-off. Water in the early morning or evening. Avoid watering when sun is shining on leaves, otherwise they will scorch; this is a particular problem with begonias.

Deadhead regularly.

Give a fortnightly liquid feed to all long-term summer flowering containers which have been overwintered.

Move houseplants outside.

Watch out for signs of slug and snail damage, vine weevil beetles, lily beetles on lilies, greenfly and blackfly, and act as necessary.

Enjoy roses, mid season clematis, ornamental grasses, herbaceous plants, all the tender bedding plants such as lobelia, busy lizzies, pelargoniums and fuchsias.

Harvest salad leaves, peas, courgettes and herb leaves.

Late Summer

Make sure your pots are kept moist and water as necessary (succulents should be kept on the dry side). Always water at soil level to avoid run-off. Water in the early morning or evening. Avoid watering when sun is shining on leaves, otherwise they will scorch; this is a particular problem with begonias.

Deadhead regularly.

Give a fortnightly liquid feed to all long-term summer flowering containers which have been overwintered.

Watch out for signs of slug and snail damage, vine weevil grubs, lily beetle grubs on lilies, greenfly and blackfly, and act as necessary.

Enjoy begonias, lilies, agapanthus, eucomis, late-flowering clematis, grasses, herbaceous plants and tender bedding plants.

Harvest tomatoes, beans, peas, cucumbers.

AUTUMN AND EARLY WINTER

Early Autumn

Begin to water less (succulents anyway should be kept on the dry side). Always water at soil level to avoid run-off. Water in the early morning or evening. Avoid watering when sun is shining on leaves, otherwise they will scorch; this is a particular problem with begonias.

Deadhead regularly.

Give a liquid feed to all long-term autumn flowering containers.

Watch out for signs of slug and snail damage, vine weevil grubs, lily beetle grubs on lilies, greenfly and blackfly, and act as necessary. Beware sudden night frosts and take precautions by bringing pots of tender plants into the greenhouse, or by covering them with newspaper or light plant membrane.

Buy miniature cyclamen, winter and spring flowering bulbs to plant in autumn. Plant winter flowering bulbs; the others can be planted now or left until mid or late autumn. Keep dry and cool until planting.

Enjoy begonias, cannas, grasses, herbaceous plants and tender bedding plants. Many will be in glorious colour.

Harvest tomatoes, beans, courgettes, aubergines, peppers, chillis, etc.

Mid Autumn

Bring all long-term tender pots into a greenhouse for winter protection. Succulents and house plants can be brought inside the home.

Cut back cannas to within 15cm of soil level.

Trim back pots of pelargoniums, fuchsias, scaevolas and other herbaceous bedding plants; there is no need to water them at this stage.

Discard annuals such as busy lizzies, petunias and lobelia.

Empty and wash pots ready for autumn planting of bulbs.

Buy miniature cyclamen and spring flowering bulbs to plant now. Choose your colour schemes, adding violas, pansies, forget-me-nots, wallflowers and ivies.

Enjoy your miniature cyclamen display, nerines, grasses and the hardy evergreens such as mahonia, holly, *Viburnum tinus*, ferns and ivies.

Late Autumn and Early Winter

Indoors

Keep a watchful eye on the greenhouse, opening it up for a while on sunny days to increase ventilation, but closing by early afternoon.

If frosts are severe you will need to add night-time heat to maintain frost-free conditions. Remove dead stems as begonias dry off.

Pick up any dead leaves from fuchsias, solanum, lantana and eucomis.

Outdoors

Move any pots with frost-hardy plants against a south-facing wall and cover with bubble wrap or fleece in severe weather. If you want to plant up small groups of snowdrops or winter flowering aconites from your garden, then dig down to find the growing bulbs and pot them up.

Enjoy your miniature cyclamen display, hardy grasses and the hardy evergreens such as mahonia, holly, *Viburnum tinus*, ferns and ivies.

USEFUL ADDRESSES

Fruit
Reads Nursery, Hales Hall, Loddon, Norfolk
NR14 6QW
Tel: 01508 548 395
www.readsnursery.co.uk

Herbs
Jekka's Herb Farm, Rose Cottage, Shellards Lane,
Alveston, Bristol BS35 3SY
Tel: 01454 418878
www.jekkasherbfarm.com

Lemons
Mare Hill Nurseries West Mare Lane,
Pulborough, West Sussex RH20 2EA
Tel: 01798 872 786
www.citruscentre.co.uk

Vegetables
Seeds of Italy Ltd., A1 Phoenix Ind. Estate,
Rosslyn Crescent, Harrow, Middlesex, HA1 2SP
Tel: 0208 427 5020
www.seedsofitaly.com

Seeds for ornamental plants and vegetables
www.thompson-morgan.com
Tel: 0844 2485 383

Bamboos
'Sunnyside', Heath Road, Kenninghall, Norfolk
NR16 2DS
Tel: (01953) 888212
www.hardybamboo.com

Ornamental grasses
Knoll Gardens, Hampreston, Wimborne
BH21 7ND
Tel: 01202 873931
www.knollgardens.co.uk

Clematis
Thorncroft Clematis Nursery, The Lings,
Reymerston, Norfolk NR9 4QG
Tel: 01953 850 407
www.thorncroftclematis.co.uk

Olives
Carodoc Doy, PO Box 28, Topsham, Exeter,
Devon EX3 0WY
Tel: 01392 877225
www.caradocdoy.co.uk

Bulbs
Walkers Bulbs, Washway House Farm, Washway
Road, Holbeach, Lincs PE12 7PP
Tel: 01406 426216
www.bulbs.co.uk

Wooden trellis planters and obelisk
Eagle Farm, Wavendon, Buckinghamshire
MK17 8AX
Tel: 07779 585 324
www.henryrichardson.co.uk

Wooden vegetable planters
(including 'A' frame, ladder, bookshelf planter,
manger and raised table)
Harrod Horticultural, Pinbush Road, Lowestoft,
Suffolk NR33 7NL
Tel: (sales) 0845 402 5300, (customer services)
0845 218 5301
www.harrodhorticultural.com

Photography
www.vanessakayphotography.co.uk
www.kathybrowngarden.com

INDEX